William Treat

Angel Voices

Or, Words of Counsel for Overcoming the World

William Treat

Angel Voices
Or, Words of Counsel for Overcoming the World

ISBN/EAN: 9783744726412

Printed in Europe, USA, Canada, Australia, Japan

Cover: Foto ©Thomas Meinert / pixelio.de

More available books at **www.hansebooks.com**

Angel Voices

OR

WORDS OF COUNSEL

for Overcoming the World.

"The soul is cured of its maladies by certain incantations: these incantations are beautiful reasons, from which temperance is generated in souls."
— SOCRATES.

"These things have I spoken unto you, that in me ye might have peace. In the world ye shall have tribulation: but be of good cheer, *I have overcome the world.*"
— MESSIAS.

A NEW AND ENLARGED EDITION.

BOSTON
Ticknor and Fields
1864

Entered according to Act of Congress, in the year 1863, by
TICKNOR AND FIELDS,
in the Clerk's Office of the District Court for the District of Massachusetts.

UNIVERSITY PRESS:
WELCH, BIGELOW, AND COMPANY,
CAMBRIDGE.

TO THOSE

WHO HAVE GIVEN

THEIR BEST AND DEAREST

FOR GOD'S WORK IN OUR COUNTRY'S CAUSE,

𝔗𝔥𝔦𝔰 𝔅𝔬𝔬𝔨

IS DEDICATED.

„Streut eifrig in empfängliche Gemüther
 Des Guten und des Schönen Samenkörner!
 Sie keimen und erblühen dort zu Bäumen,
 Die goldne Paradiesesfrüchte tragen."

ANGEL VOICES.

INDEX OF AUTHORS AND WORKS QUOTED.

[The numbers correspond with those in the text.]

0 Unknown.
1 Lyra Innocentium.
2 Festus.
3 Quarles.
4 Alfred Tennyson.
5 Whittier.
6 Mrs. Jameson.
7 Mrs. Silsbee.
8 Goethe.
9 Rahel.
10 Montgomery.
11 Mrs. Child.
12 J. R. Lowell.
13 D. A. Wasson.
14 R. Browning.
15 Emerson.
16 Bishop Hall.
17 Milton.
18 Sir Thomas Browne.
19 Coleridge.
20 Bishop Taylor.
21 John Bunyan.
22 C. A. Bartol.
23 Thomas à Kempis.
24 Tragedy of Errors.
25 A. Bronson Alcott.
26 Edmund Waller.
27 William Treat.
28 Spenser.
29 Barry Cornwall.
30 Victor Hugo.
31 Dryden.
32 Portsmouth Journal.
33 Harriet Martineau.
34 Jean Paul Friedrich Richter.
35 William Wordsworth.
36 Thomas Carlyle.
37 Plato.
38 Keats.
39 Schiller.
40 Dr. Fuller.
41 Dr. John Brown.
42 Jones Very.
43 Essays written in Intervals of Business.
44 Chaucer.
45 Bettina.
46 Dr. Samuel Brown.
47 John James Taylor.
48 Saadi.
49 Helps.
50 Shakespeare.
51 Akenside.
52 Camoens.
53 North British Review.
54 Vaughan.
55 Bacon, Lord Verulam.
56 Patience of Hope.
57 William Ware.
58 Cornelius Matthews.
59 Fénelon.
60 Feltham.
61 Young's Night Thoughts.
62 Herder.
63 Kingsley.
64 Christian Examiner.
65 W. S. Landor.
66 N. P. Willis.
67 Confucius.
68 Economy of Life (A.D. 1800).
69 Thomas De Quincey.
70 Dr. Wadsworth.
71 Francis de Sales.
72 Longfellow.
73 Offering of Sympathy.
74 Charles Lamb.
75 Arthur Hallam.
76 George Herbert.
77 Milnes.
78 F. Schlegel.
79 Barrow.
80 James Martineau.
81 Ruskin.
82 Sismondi.
83 Thomas Hood.
84 Henry Giles.
85 W. C. Bryant.
86 Mountford.
87 Dickens.
88 Edward Jarvis.
89 Henry Taylor.
90 Dr. Watts.
91 Lamartine.
92 Pope.
93 Thackeray.
94 The Dial.

ANGEL VOICES.

95 Archytes on the Good and Happy Man.
96 Dr. Parr.
97 Shelley.
98 Sterling.
99 Hare.
100 Chapman.
101 William Dunbar.
102 Thomas Decker.
103 Crashaw.
104 Jacobi.
105 Hymns of the Ages.
106 Sir William Temple.
107 Dr. Walker.
108 Thoreau.
109 Sidney Smith.
110 Wilkinson.
111 Hippodamus on Felicity.
112 Pascal.
113 Cecil.
114 J. H. Thom.
115 A. L. Waring.
116 Seed-Grain.
117 Thomas C. Upham.
118 Lyra Germanica.
119 Story of To-day.
120 Reminiscences of Thought and Feeling.
121 E. H. Sears.
122 Lady Elizabeth Carew.
123 Leigh Hunt.
124 Thomson.
125 Clough.
126 Dürer's Artist's Married Life.
127 Mrs. Stowe.
128 Benjamin Whichcote.
129 Shirley.
130 W. Irving.
131 R. C. Waterston.
132 W. E. Channing.
133 Morison.
134 Parting Gift.
135 Fields.
136 Dr. South.
137 Chambers's Journal.
138 Sir Walter Raleigh.
139 Webster.
140 Baxter.
141 Spanish of Argensolas.
142 Dr. Dewey.
143 John Wilson.
144 Gerald Massey.
145 H. W. Beecher.
146 Breviary.
147 F. W. Robertson.
148 O. W. Holmes
149 Maria Lowell.
150 Mrs. Browning.
151 A. A. Procter.
152 Cowper.
153 Russian Poetry.
154 G. W. Bethune.
155 W. D. Moir.
156 Sir John Davies.
157 Williams.
158 Leopold Schefer.
159 Edmeston.
160 Dr. W. E. Channing.
161 G. W. Doane.
162 Thomas Aird.
163 Vita Nuova.
164 F. W. Newman.
165 Robert Nicoll.
166 Constant.
167 Habington.
168 Giles Fletcher.
169 Dirk Smits.
170 Dublin University Magazine.
171 Jacob Boehme.
172 Gaskill.
173 J. F. Clarke.
174 Author of "Counterparts" and "Charles Auchester."
175 Marcus Antoninus.

Fear not to approach!

I here present thee with a hive of Bees, laden some with wax and some with honey.

There are no Wasps, there are no Hornets here.

THERE are who love upon their knees
To linger when their prayers are said,
And lengthen out their Litanies,
In duteous care for quick and dead.
Thou of all Love the Source and Guide!
O may some hovering thought of theirs,
Where I am kneeling, gently glide,
And higher waft these earth-bound prayers.

Thus may the heart of Innocents
On earth, of Saints in heaven above,
Guard, as of old, our lonely tents,
Till, as one Faith is ours, in Love
We own all Churches, and are owned;
Thus may He save, by chastenings keen,
The harps that hail His Bride enthroned,
From wayward touch of hands unclean.[1]

PRELUDE.

—

REMEMBER,

These are "Reminiscences of the best hours of Life for the hour of Death," by which we may look back from the glow of the evening to the brightness of the morning of Youth. "Give me," said Herder to his son, as he lay in the parched weariness of his last illness,— "give me a great thought, that I may quicken myself with it." Let these thoughts, whether they come in the best hours of life, or in the hour of death, teach

> Each man to think himself an act of God,
> His mind a thought, his life a breath of God;
> And bid each try, by great thoughts and good deeds,
> To show the most of Heaven he hath in him.[2]

PART 1.

OF LIFE.

Think not, Earth, that I would raise
Weary forehead in thy praise,
(Weary that I cannot go
Farther from thy region low,)
If were struck no richer meanings
From thee than thyself.

Praised be the mosses soft
In thy forest pathways oft,
And the thorns, which make us think
Of the thornless river-brink,
  Where the ransomed tread.
Praised be thy sunny gleams,
And the storm that worketh dreams
  Of calm unfinishèd.
Praised be thine active days,
And thy night-time's solemn need,
When in God's dear book we read,
No night shall be therein.

Earth, we Christians praise thee thus,
Even for the change that comes
With a grief from thee to us!
For thy cradles and thy tombs,
For the pleasant corn and wine,
And summer heat; and also for
The frost upon the sycamore,
And hail upon the vine!

The Angels in like manner can utter in a few words singular the things which are written in a volume of any book, and can express such things, or every word, as elevate its meaning to interior wisdom; for their speech is such, that it is consonant with affections, and every word with ideas. Expressions are also varied, by an infinity of methods, according to the series of the things which are in a complex in the thought.— SWEDENBORG.

> Our echoes roll from soul to soul,
> And grow forever and forever.[4]

Being tempted: Angels ministered unto him.

ANGEL VOICES.

 To weary hearts, to mourning homes,
God's meekest angel gently comes;
No power has he to banish pain,
Or give us back our lost again;
And yet in tenderest love our dear
And Heavenly Father sends him here.[5]

REMEMBER,

 Blessed is the memory of those who have kept themselves unspotted *from* the world! Yet more blessed and more dear the memory of those who have kept themselves unspotted *in* the world.[6]

 Eyes, that with holy tears are dim,
Shine, when God's sunbeam on them plays;
In stricken souls angelic lays
Are rising like a happy hymn.

 And friends belovèd, unto whom
Sorrow hath come with keenest sting
The drooping of the angel's wing
Shall bring the shade and not the gloom.[7]

Blessed are the poor in spirit.

REMEMBER,

True religion teaches us to reverence what is under us, to recognize humility and poverty, and, despite mockery and disgrace, wretchedness, suffering, and death, as things divine.[9]

> The saint that wears heaven's brightest crown
> In deepest adoration bends;
> The weight of glory bows him down
> Then most when most his soul ascends;
>   Nearest the throne itself must be
>   The footstool of humility.[10]

REMEMBER,

So long as we do not take even the injustice which is done us, and which forces the burning tears from us, — so long as we do not take even this for just and right, we are in the thickest darkness without dawn.[9]

> The bird that soars on highest wing
> Builds on the ground her lowly nest;
> And she that does most sweetly sing
> Sings in the shade when all things rest;
>   In lark and nightingale we see
>   What honor hath humility.[10]

REMEMBER,

The mere lapse of years is not life: to eat

I am that Bread of Life.

and drink and sleep; to be exposed to the darkness and the light; to pace round in the mill of habit, and turn the wheel of wealth; to make reason our book-keeper, and turn thought into an implement of trade, — this is not life. In all this, but a poor fraction of the consciousness of humanity is awakened; and the sanctities still slumber which make it most worth while to be. Knowledge, truth, love, beauty, goodness, faith, alone give vitality to the mechanism of existence.

The laugh of mirth that vibrates through the heart, the tears that freshen the dry wastes within, the music that brings childhood back, the prayer that calls the future near, the doubt which makes us meditate, the death which startles us with mystery, the hardship which forces us to struggle, the anxiety that ends in trust, are the true nourishment of our natural being.[10]

> We live in deeds, not years; in thoughts, not breaths;
> In feelings, not in figures on a dial.
> We should count time by heart-throbs. He most lives
> Who thinks most, feels the noblest, acts the best;
> And he whose heart beats quickest lives the longest,
> Lives in one hour more than in years do some

He that eateth of this bread shall live forever.

Whose fat blood sleeps, as it slips along their veins.
Life is but a means unto an end ; that end,
Beginning, mean, and end to all things — God.
The dead have all the glory of the world.[2]

REMEMBER

The wealth of a man is the number of things which he loves and blesses, which he is loved and blessed by.

..... For amid all life's guests
There seems but worthy one — to do men good ;
It matters not how long we live, but how ;
For as the parts of one mankind while here,
We live in every age.[2]

REMEMBER.

This, and especially the type which follows ; place it securely among the multitude of wares in the store-house of "beautiful memories."

There is a fine engraving of Jean Paul Richter, surrounded by floating clouds, all of which are angels' faces ; but so soft and shadowy, that they must be sought for, to be perceived. It was a beautiful idea thus to environ Jean Paul, for whosoever reads him with earnest thoughtfulness will see heavenly features perpetually shining forth through the golden mists or rolling vapor. ..... Remember, — This picture embodies a great spiritual

Praise the Lord, O my soul, and forget not all his benefits.

truth. In all clouds that surround the soul, there *are* angel faces, and we should *see* them if we were calm and holy. It is because we are impatient of our destiny, and do not understand its use in our eternal progression, that the clouds which envelop it seem like black masses of thunder, or cold and dismal obstructions of the sunshine. If man looked at his being as a whole, or had faith that all things were intended to bring him into harmony with the Divine will, he would gratefully acknowledge that spiritual dew and rain, wind and lightning, cloud and sunshine, all help his growth, as their natural forms bring to maturity the flowers and the grain. "Whosoever quarrels with his fate does not understand it," says Bettine; and among all her inspired sayings, she spoke none wiser."

> High natures must be thunder-scarred
> With many a searing wrong;
> Naught unmarred with struggles hard
> Can make the soul's sinews strong.[12]

Remember.

Dante places in his lowest Hell those who in life were melancholy and repining without a cause, thus profaning and darkening God's blessed sunshine, — "Tristi fummo nel aer dolce"; and in some of the ancient Christian systems of virtues and vices, melancholy is unholy and a vice; cheerfulness is holy and a virtue.

Lord Bacon also makes one of the characteristics of moral health and goodness to consist in "a quick sense of felicity and a noble satisfaction."

What moments, hours, days, of exquisite felicity must Christ our Redeemer have had, though it has become too customary to place him before us only in the attitude of pain and sorrow! Why should he be always crowned with thorns, bleeding with wounds, weeping over the world he was appointed to heal, to save, to reconcile with God? The radiant head of Christ in Raphael's "Transfiguration" should rather be our ideal of Him who came to "bind up the broken-hearted, to preach the acceptable year of the Lord."

"All mine is thine," the sky-soul saith:
"The wealth I am, must thou become:
Richer and richer breath by breath, —
Immortal gain, immortal room!"
And since all his
Mine also is,
Life's gift outruns my fancies far,
And drowns the dream
In larger stream,
As morning drinks the morning star."

ANGEL VOICES. 17

That he who loveth God love his brother also.

Remember,

Inquiringly, — If we float over the surface of society with perpetual sunshine and favoring airs, how can we sound the shoals and gulf which lie below?[6]

Night brings out stars, as sorrow shows us truths.[2]

Remember,

By earnest endeavor, to gladden the human circle in which we live, — to open our hearts to the gospel of life and nature, seizing each moment and the good which it brings, be it friendly glance, spring breeze, or flower, extracting from every moment a drop of the honey of eternal life.[12]

"True bliss is to be found in holy life;
In charity to men, and love to God."

Probe the profound of thine own nature, Man!
And thou may'st see reflected, e'en in life,
The worlds, the heavens, the ages; by and by,
The coming come.[2]

Remember,

That unto him who works, and feels he works,
This same *grand year* is ever at the doors.

Remember,

Those who would understand the courses of the heavens above, must first of all recognize the heaven in men.

Blessed are the merciful.

Remember.

There is a law of neutralization of forces, which hinders bodies from sinking beyond a certain depth in the sea; but in the ocean of baseness, the deeper we get, the easier the sinking. As for the kindness which Milton and Burns felt for the Devil, I am sure that God thinks of him with pity a thousand times to their once, and the good Origen believed him not incapable of salvation.[12]

Remember.

Mercy is

> mightiest in the mightiest; it becomes
> The thronèd monarch better than his crown;
> His sceptre shows the force of temporal power,
> The attribute to awe and majesty,
> Wherein doth sit the dread and fear of kings;
> But mercy is above this sceptred sway,
> It is enthronèd in the hearts of kings;
> It is an attribute to God himself.[30]

Remember.

There never was a right endeavor but it succeeded. Patience and patience, we shall win at the last. We must be very suspicious of the deceptions and elements of time. It takes a good deal of time to eat or to sleep, or to earn a hundred dollars, and a very little time to entertain a hope and an insight which

Blessed are they that hunger and thirst after righteousness:

becomes the light of our life; — daily routine makes but little impression; but in the solitude to which every man is always returning, he has a sanity and revelations, which in his passage into new worlds he will carry with him.[13] Thus may

"Our yesterdays look backward with a smile."

REMEMBER,

The simplest faith, be it only deep and trustful, the very smallest idea of a mission in life assigned by God, — be it only lovingly and clearly seen, — "lifteth the poor out of the dust," and "to them that have no might increaseth strength." As of old it banished disease, and couched the blind, and soothed the maniac, by miracles of power, so does it still heal and bless by its miracles of love. It puts a divine fire into the dullest soul, and draws in Saul also among the prophets; it turns the peasant into the apostle, and the apostle's meanest follower into the martyr.[8]

.....all ambitious upwards tending,
Like plants in mines, which never saw the sun,
But dream of him, and guess where he may be,
They do their best to climb, and get to him.[14]

REMEMBER,

There do remain dispersed in the soil of

They shall be filled.

human nature divers seeds of goodness, of benignity, of ingenuity, which being cherished, excited, and quickened by good culture, do, by common experience, thrust out flowers very lovely, and yield fruits very pleasant of virtue and goodness."

Good deeds are very fruitful. Out of one good action of ours, God produces a thousand; the harvest whereof is perpetual. If good deeds were utterly barren and incommodious, I would seek after them from a consciousness of their own goodness; how much more shall I now be encouraged to perform them, that they are so profitable both to myself and others?[16] Since men may,

> "after all their tribulations long,
> See golden days fruitful of golden deeds,
> With joy and peace triumphing, and fair truth."[17]

REMEMBER.

There is no felicity in that the earth adores. That wherein God himself is happy, the holy angels are happy, in whose defect the devils are unhappy, — that dare I call happiness. Whatsoever conduceth unto this may, with an easy metaphor, deserve that name. Whatsoever else the world terms happiness is to me a story out of Pliny, a tale of Boccace or Ma-

As he prayed, his countenance was altered.

lizspini, an apparition or a neat delusion, wherein there is no more of happiness than the name. Bless me in this life with but peace of my conscience, command of my affections, the love of my dearest friends, and I shall be happy enough to pity Cæsar. These are, O Lord, the humble desires of my most reasonable ambition, and all I dare call happiness on earth ; wherein I set no rule or limit to thy hand of providence. Dispose of me according to the wisdom of thy pleasure. Thy will be done, though in my undoing.[18]

REMEMBER,

Believing with me, to pray with all your heart and strength, with the reason and the will, to believe vividly that God will listen to your voice through Christ, and verily do the thing he pleaseth thereupon,—that is the last, the greatest achievement of the Christian's warfare on earth.[19]

> He prayeth well who loveth well
> Both man and bird and beast.
>
> He prayeth best who loveth best
> All things both great and small ;
> For the same God who loveth us,
> He made and loveth all.[19]

Blessed are the pure in heart.

Remember,

Prayers are but the body of the bird; desires are its angel's wings.[20]

> In the greatest battle of his life
> Man stands by himself alone;
> No hand save his and the foes to the strife,
> No heart to beat high but his own.
>
> Yet the war goes on right desperately,
> And whether he stand or fall
> Himself and God alone may see
> Till the judgment-day of all.

Remember,

In prayer it is better to have a heart without words, than words without a heart.[21]

Therefore let every man study his prayers, and read his duty in his petitions. For the body of our prayer is the sum of our duty; and as we must ask of God whatsoever we need, so we must labor for all that we ask.[22]

> More things are wrought by prayer
> Than this world dreams of. Wherefore let thy voice
> Rise like a fountain for me night and day;
> For what are men better than sheep or goats,
> That nourish a blind life within the brain,
> If, knowing God, they lift not hands of prayer,
> Both for themselves and those who call them friend?
> For so the whole round world is every way
> Bound by gold chains about the feet of God.[4]

They shall see God.

REMEMBER,

The making one object, in outward or inward nature, more holy to a single heart, is reward enough for a life; for the more sympathies we gain or awaken for what is beautiful, by so much deeper will be our sympathy for that which is most beautiful, — the human soul.[12]

> Those there are
> Whose hearts have a look southward, and are open
> To the whole noon of nature.
> Be thou of such.[3]

REMEMBER.

"Who are the most godlike of men? The question might be a puzzling one unless our language answered it for us, — the godliest."

> Thou, O Spirit, that dost prefer
> Before all temples the upright heart and pure,
> Instruct me.[17]

REMEMBER.

Only the Purified are the Pure.[22]

REMEMBER.

It is only the finite that has wrought and suffered; the infinite lies stretched in smiling repose.[15]

> God is the Perfect Poet,
> Who in creation acts his own conceptions.

Become as little children.

> Shall man refuse to be aught else than God?
> Man's weakness is his glory, — for the strength
> Which raises him to Heaven and near God's self
> Came spite of it; God's strength his glory is,
> For thence came with our weakness sympathy,
> Which brought God down to earth a man like us.[14]

When a man is so far advanced in the Christian life, as not to seek consolation from any created thing, then does he first begin perfectly to enjoy God; then "in whatsoever state he is, he will therewith be content"; then neither can prosperity exalt, nor adversity depress him, but his heart is wholly fixed and established in God, who is his All in All.[23]

Then

> Love is a celestial harmony.[50]

> His thoughts were as a pyramid up-piled,
> On whose far top an angel stood and smiled,
> Yet in his heart he was a little child.

REMEMBER,

> Wisdom, earthly wisdom
> Is the last wealth a man can take to heaven:
> More cumbersome it is than bags of gold.
> . . . .
> And would you know what station God prefers,
> And what respect he has for human learning,
> Inquire where Christ was born, and what his breeding.[24]

REMEMBER.

Whoever speaks not to the love and wonder

Blessed is the man that maketh the Lord his trust.

of mankind, says little deserving of lasting interest.[25]

> For all we know
> Of what the blessed do above
> Is that they sing, and that they love.[26]

REMEMBER

Schiller's words; they are to the mother of young Carlos. "Tell him, that when become a man he shall reverence the dreams of his youth, that he shall not open his heart, the tender, divine flower, to the deathly insect of boasted superior wisdom."

REMEMBER.

Only a great pride, that is, a great and reverential repose in one's own being, renders possible a noble humility.[13]

REMEMBER,

If the will, which is the law of our nature, were withdrawn from our memory, fancy, understanding, and reason, no other hell could equal, for a spiritual being, what we should then feel, from the anarchy of our powers. It would be conscious madness, — a horrid thought!"

REMEMBER,

Man cannot be *utterly* lost to good, for then

Labor not for the meat which perisheth.

he would be a devil at once. Thus to talk is absurd."[19] Even Montgomery's "Satan,"

> Though by nature a whirlpool of desires,
> And mighty passions, perilously mixed,
> Yet, with the darkness of the demon world,
> Had he something of the light of heaven.

REMEMBER,

That victory belongs to him who is constant in faith and courage. That Peter, by faith, walked upon the water, until, momentarily losing his faith, he began to sink. A history, Goethe said, he loved better than any; as it expresses the noble doctrine that man, through faith and animated courage, may come off victor in the most dangerous enterprises, while he may be ruined by a momentary paroxysm of doubt."[27]

REMEMBER,

He hath riches sufficient who hath enough to be charitable.[18]

And forget not, that Mammon was

> "the least erected Spirit that fell
> From heaven; for even in heaven his looks and thoughts
> Were always downward bent; admiring more
> The riches of heaven's pavement, trodden gold,
> Than aught divine or holy else enjoyed
> In vision beatific."[17]

Poor and content is rich.[50]

Thou art my rock.

      I do rather choose
To be the lord of those that riches have,
Than have them to myself and be their servile slave.[28]

REMEMBER,
Everything perishes except Truth, and the worship of Truth, and Poetry, which is its enduring language.[29]

 "Rich are the diligent, who can command
 Time, nature's stock! and could his hour-glass fall,
 Would, as for seed of stars, stoop for the sand,
 And by incessant labor gather all."

REMEMBER,
It is only the stout heart, and strong, resolute will, that enables one in truth to say,

    This life of mine
 Must be lived out, and a grave thoroughly earned.

    Pitch then thy project high:
 Sink not in spirit. Who aimeth at the sky
 Shoots higher much than if he meant a tree.
 Let thy mind still be bent, still plotting where,
 And when, and how, the business may be done.[76]

L'Enfant chantait; la mère au lit, exténuée,
Agonisait, beau front dans l'ombre se penchant;
La Mort au dessus d'elle errait dans la nuée,
Et j'ecoutais ce râle, et j'entendait ce chant.

L'Enfant avait cinq ans et près de la fenêtre,
Ses rires et ses jeux faisaient un charmant bruit;
Et la mère à côté de ce pauvre doux être
Qui chantait tout le jour, toussait toute la nuit.

Jesus opened his mouth and taught them.

La mère alla dormir sous les dalles du cloître :
Et le petit enfant se remit à chanter. . . . . .
· La douleur est un fruit ; Dieu ne le fait pas croître
Sur la branche trop faible encore pour le porter.[30]

REMEMBER,

In joy and affliction, and resolve with Siebenkäs: " It is thy intention to try my soul, good Destiny, and therefore dost thou put it into every position, as a man does his watch, into a perpendicular and a horizontal position, easy and uneasy ones, in order to see whether it goes well, and shows the time correctly. Verily it shall!"[34]

Greatness and goodness are not means, but ends ;
Hath he not always treasures, always friends,
The good, great man? Three treasures — Love and Light,
And calm Thoughts, regular as infant's breath : —
And three firm friends, more sure than day and night,
Himself, his *Maker*, and the *Angel Death*.[19]

REMEMBER,

Speech is the light, the morning of the mind ;
It spreads the beauteous images abroad,
Which else lie furled and shrouded in the soul.[31]

Life is a suggestion of the Spirit through the mind, giving us news of Him in guise of queries for beginners in the study of it.[25]

REMEMBER,

A child should be approached with rever-

Is it not written in your law, I said, Ye are gods?

ence as a recipient of the Spirit from above. The best of books claims the best of persons and the gracious moments to make its meaning clear, else the reading and listening are but a sounding pretence, and of no account. The Spirit within must invite and prepare the heart instantly, — inspiration answer inspiration, and so answering, informing and renewing; a Pentecost and an awakening from on high. I have wished these books were opened with the awe belonging to the eminent personalities portrayed therein, thinking them best read when the glow of the sentiment kindles the meaning into life.[25]

Yet forget not that, the man who cannot enjoy his own natural gifts in silence, and find his reward in the exercise of them, will generally find himself badly off.[8]

Remember.
The eloquent man is he who is no eloquent speaker, but who is inwardly drunk with a certain belief.[15]

Remember.
"As no man liveth to himself," so no man sinneth to himself; and every vagrant habit uprooted from the young and ignorant — ev-

I have declared thy faithfulness and thy salvation.

ery principle of duty strengthened — every encouragement to reform offered, and rightly persevered in — is casting a shield of safety over the property, life, peace, and every true interest of community ; so that it may be said of this most emphatically, as of every duty of man, " Knowing these things, *happy are ye if ye do them.*" [32]

>Beneath this starry arch,
> Naught resteth or is still ;
>But all things hold their march,
> As if by one great will.
>   Moves one, move all :
>   Hark to the footfall !
>   On, on, forever !
>
>Yon sheaves were once but seed :
>Will ripens into deed ;
>As eave-drops swell the streams,
>Day thoughts feed nightly dreams ;
>And sorrow tracketh wrong,
>As echo follows song,
> On, on, forever !
>
>By night, like stars on high,
> The hours reveal their train ;
>They whisper, and go by,
> "I never watch in vain."
>   Moves one, move all :
>   Hark to the footfall !
>   On, on, forever !

If we love one another, God dwelleth in us.

>They pass the cradle-head,
>And there a promise shed;
>They pass the moist new grave,
>And bid rank verdure wave;
>They bear through every clime
>The harvests of all time,
>   On, on, forever![33]

REMEMBER,

If thy heart yearns for love, *be* loving; if thou wouldst free mankind *be* free; if thou wouldst have a brother frank to thee, *be* frank to him: "But what will people say?" — Eternal and sure is this promise, "Blessed are the meek, for they shall inherit the earth." Only have faith in this, and thou wilt live high above the rewards and punishments of that *spectral giant*, which men call *Society*. Be found with thine own conscience in that circle of duties, which widens ever, till it enfolds all beings and touches the throne of God."

>Be noble! and the nobleness that lies
>In other men, *sleeping*, but never *dead*,
>Will rise in majesty to meet thine own.[b]

REMEMBER.

To think gently of all, and include all without exception in the circle of our kindly sympathies, not thrusting out even the common hangman (though if athirst, I should prefer

What God hath cleansed, that call not thou common.

receiving water, if it required waiting, from other hands than his). Yet what is the hangman but a servant of public opinion? And what is the law but an expression of public opinion? And if public opinion is brutal, and thou a component part thereof, art thou not the hangman's accomplice? In the name of our common Father, sing thy part of the great chorus in the truest time, and thus bring this crashing discord into harmony.[12]

> Man is dear to man: the poorest poor
> Long for some moments in a weary life
> When they can know and feel that they have been
> Themselves the fathers and the dealers out
> Of some small blessings; have been kind to such
> As needed kindness, *for this single cause,*
> That we have all of us one human heart.[35]

REMEMBER,

Drinking, singing, talking, none of these things are good in themselves, but the mode in which they are done stamps them with its own nature; and that which is done well is good, and that which is done ill is evil.[37]

REMEMBER,

Rightly viewed, no object is insignificant; all objects are as windows, through which the philosophic eye looks into infinitude itself.

ANGEL VOICES. 33

How beautiful are thy works!

    Now, if this earthly love has power to make
    Men's being mortal, immortal; to shake
    Ambition from their memories, and brim
    Their measure of content; what merest whim
    Seems all this poor endeavor after fame
    To one, who keeps within his steadfast aim
    A love immortal, an immortal too.[38]

        Howe'er it be, it seems to me
        'T is only noble to be good;
        Kind hearts are more than coronets
        And simple faith than Norman blood.[4]

REMEMBER.

    It is only through the morning gate of the beautiful that you can penetrate into the realm of knowledge. That which we feel here as beauty, we shall one day know as truth.[39]

            His grave rebuke,
      Severe in youthful beauty, added grace
      Invincible: abashed the Devil stood,
      And felt how awful goodness is, and saw
      Virtue in her shape, how lovely.[17]

REMEMBER.

    That a beautiful form is better than a beautiful face; a beautiful behavior is better than a beautiful form; it gives a higher pleasure than statues or pictures; it is the finest of the fine arts.[15]

Sing unto the Lord a new song.

> The idea of her life shall sweetly creep
> Into his study of imagination;
> And every lovely organ of her life
> Shall come apparelled in more precious habit,
> More moving delicate, and full of life,
> Into the eye and prospect of his soul,
> Than when she lived indeed.[50]

REMEMBER,

Upon sight of beautiful persons, to bless God in his creatures, to pray for the beauty of their souls, and to enrich them with inward graces to be answerable unto the outward. Upon sight of deformed persons, to send them inward graces, and enrich their souls, and give them the beauty of the resurrection.[18]

REMEMBER,

In thankfulness, thy Heavenly Father, for every manifestation of human love. Thank him for all experiences, be they sweet or bitter, which help to forgive all things and enfold the whole world with blessing. "What shall be our reward," asks Swedenborg, "for loving our neighbor *as* ourselves in this life? That when we become angels, we shall be enabled to love *him* better than ourselves." This is a reward pure and holy; the only one which my heart has not rejected, whenever offered as an incitement to goodness. It is this which,

O that men would praise the Lord for his goodness.

chiefly, makes the happiness of lovers more nearly allied to heaven than any other emotions experienced by the human heart. Each loves the other better than self; each is willing to sacrifice all to the other, nay, finds joy therein. This is it that surrounds them with a golden atmosphere, and tinges the world with rose-color. A mother's love has the same angelic character; more completely unselfish, but lacking the charm of perfect reciprocity."

Neither shalt thou forget thy song, when, as Bettine has said, "The whole country looks as if it had turned its face towards its Creator."

> Heaven "disapproves that care, though wise in show,
> That with superfluous burden loads the day,
> And when God sends a cheerful hour, refrains."[17]

Remember.

"Gratitude is memory of the heart." Therefore forget not to say often, with Bettine, "I have all I have ever enjoyed."

Remember.

If thou beest not so handsome as thou wouldest have been, thank God thou art no more unhandsome than thou art. It is his mercy thou art not the mark for passengers'

Seek not honor one of another.

fingers to point at, a heteroclite in nature with some member defective or redundant. Be glad that thy clay cottage hath all the necessary rooms thereto belonging, though the outside be not so fairly plastered as some others.[40]

REMEMBER,

You must in a certain sense *reward* God. You cannot give him money, for the silver and gold, the cattle upon a thousand hills, are all his already, but you can give him your grateful lives; you can give him your hearts; and, as old Mr. Henry says, "Thanksgiving is good, but thanks-living is better." [41]

> It is not life upon thy gifts to live,
> But to grow fixed with deeper roots in thee;
> And when the sun and shower their bounties give,
> To send out thick-leaved limbs: a fruitful tree,
> Whose green head meets the eye for many a mile.[42]

REMEMBER.

A great deal of discomfort arises from over-sensitiveness about what people may say of you or your actions. Many unhappy persons seem to imagine that they are always in an amphitheatre, with the assembled world as spectators; whereas they are playing to empty benches all the while.[43]

If any will come after me, let him deny himself.

Fly from the prease, and dwell with soothfastnesse,
Suffice unto thy good though it be small,
For horde hath hate, and climbing tickelnesse,
Prease hath envy and wele (wealth) is blent over all,
Savour no more than thee behove shall,
Rede well thyselfe that other folke canst rede,
And trouth thee shall deliver, it is no drede.

Paine thee not ech crooked to redresse
In trust of her that tourneth as a ball,
Greate rest standeth in little businesse,
Beware also to spurn againe a nall,
Strive not as doth a crocke with a wall,
Deme thyselfe that demest others dede,
And trouth thee shall deliver, it is no drede.

That thee is sent receive in buxomnesse,
The wrestling of this world asketh a fall,
Here is no home, here is but wildernesse,
Forth, pilgrime! forth, beast, out of thy stall!
Look up on high and thanke God of all!
Forsake thy lusts, and let thy ghost thee lede
And trouth thee shall deliver, it is no drede.[44]

REMEMBER,
 The Lord creates occasions of contest, to bless us with opportunities of victory.[23]
 Who has ever loved who has reserved anything for himself? Reservation is self-love.[45]

REMEMBER,
 The unselfish must be economical.[43]

Jesus said, My kingdom is not of this world.

Remember,

The old Polytheism was Nature, in the plenitude of sensuous wealth, projecting the shadow of her gorgeous but coarse imagery on the pure expanse of the Infinite ; not the might and glory of the Infinite coming down on Nature with resistless influence, to chasten and spiritualize her wild energies, and humble them in reverent submission to the law of the Eternal. . . . . . Our intensest conviction of the presence of God, our dearest persuasion that he has drawn nigh to us, is not, however, when we are the quiet and contemplative spectators of His works, or the passive recipients of outward influence ; but in those higher exercises of faith which engage our wills, and put us on virtuous effort, and excite us to active co-operation with Him, — when we seek Him, and believe that we have found Him, in the glad appropriation of every duty and the cheerful acceptance of every sacrifice which he demands."

Remember,

That maxim is of earth, of fallible man, which says, "The voice of the people is the voice of God." It may be, but with equal probability also the voice of the Devil. That the voice of ten millions of men calling for the

He that followeth me shall not walk in darkness.

same thing is a spirit, I believe; but whether that be the spirit of heaven or hell, I can only know by trying the thing called for by the prescript of reason.[19] Even then that knowledge must be infinite, embracing the whole cycle of God's universe. Better said, by the same, "Public opinion is the average prejudices of the community."

REMEMBER,

Heaven is not separated from temporal life by an abyss that in death we must overleap; heaven begins immediately where we first feel impelled for the conception of the divine.[45]

Heaven lies about us in our infancy.[35]

REMEMBER,

The beloved of the Almighty are the rich who have the humility of the poor, and the poor who have the magnanimity of the rich.[13]

REMEMBER,

Would you make yourself dear to every domestic scene you enter, form the habit of forbearance, and all your kindred will bless your face for its own benediction. Your very coming in at the door shall be as a balm: and that comfort is not insignificant which is repeated, a drop of sweetness in every draught, a thousand and a million times.[23]

But shall have the light of life.

REMEMBER,

For thy consolation in the hurry of life, that perhaps the short hasty gazes cast up any day in the midst of business, in a dense city, at the heavens, or at a bit of tree seen amid buildings, — gazes which partake almost more of a sigh than a look, have in them more of intense appreciation of the beauties of nature than all that has been felt by an equal number of sight-seers enjoying large opportunity of seeing, and all their time to themselves. Like a prayer offered up in the midst of every-day life, these short, fond gazes at nature have something inconceivably soothing and beautiful in them.[49]

REMEMBER,

The highest and most profitable learning is the knowledge and contempt of ourselves; and to have no opinion of our own merit, and always to think well and highly of others, is an evidence of great wisdom and perfection. Why dost thou prefer thyself to another, since thou mayst find many who are more learned than thou art, and better instructed in the will of God.[23]

> The man forget not, though in rags he lies,
> And know the mortal through the crown's disguise.[51]

Of such are the kingdom of heaven.

>Just like Love is yonder rose ;
>Heavenly sweetness round it throws,
>And in the midst of briers it blows,
>Just like Love ![52]

Remember,

Life — strong life and sound life — that life which lends approaches to the Infinite, and takes hold on Heaven, is not so much a progress as it is a resistance.[53]

Why should we be cowed by the name of Action? ..... We know that the ancestor of every action is a thought...... To think is to act...... Let us, if we must have great actions, make our own so. All action is of infinite elasticity, and the least admits of being inflated with celestial air, until it eclipses the sun and moon. Let us seek one peace by fidelity. Let me do my duties. Why need I go gadding into the scenes and philosophy of Greek and Italian history, before I have washed my own face, or justified myself to my own benefactors? How dare I read Washington's campaigns, when I have not answered the letters of my own correspondents? Is not that a just objection to much of our reading? It is a pusillanimous desertion of our work to gaze after our neighbors.[15]

Martha, Martha, thou art careful and troubled about many things;

Remember,

That religion is, in its essence, the most gentlemanly thing in the world. It will, *alone and of itself*, gentilize, if unmixed with cant; and I know of nothing else that will.[19]

There is no wisdom, no perception of truth, which asks for more than to be loved.[45]

Remember,

We cannot make our home too attractive. Let it be the home of the affections; a parlor for conversation, a pantry of comforts, yet not reminding us too broadly of the brute satisfactions. Let its chambers open eastward, admitting sunshine and the sanctities, for our and still more for the children's sakes. They covet the clear sky, delighting in the blue they left so lately, nay, cannot leave in coming into Nature, whereof they are ever asking the news of it. The gay enthusiasts must run eagerly, and never have enough of it. Their poise and their plenitude rebuke us. So the poet sings sadly, yet truly for some of us[25]:—

> "Happy those early days when I
> Shined in my angel infancy;
> Before I taught my soul to wound
> My conscience with a sinful sound,
> Or taught my soul to fancy aught
> But a white celestial thought,

ANGEL VOICES. 43

But one thing is needful.

> Or had the black art to dispense
> A several sin to every sense;
> But felt through all this fleshly dress
> Bright shoots of everlastingness." [54]

REMEMBER.

Animate the heart, and it no longer thirsts for common air, but for ether. No one is less vain than a bride.[34]

REMEMBER.

Two sentiments alone suffice for man, were he to live the age of the rocks, — love, and the contemplation of the Deity.[90]

REMEMBER.

The word of Solon to Crœsus, when in ostentation he showed him his gold: "Sir, if any other come that hath better iron than you, he will be master of all this gold." [55]

REMEMBER.

The sober Christian may possibly feel a shock in finding Novalis describe his faith as a foe "to art, to science, even to enjoyment"; yet does not his own daily experience prove that the holding of the one thing needful involves the letting go of many things lovely and desirable, and that in thought as well as in action he must go on, "ever narrowing his

If there be any virtue, and if there be any praise, think on these things.

way, *avoiding much.*" And this, not because his intellect is darkened to perceive beauty and excellence, or his affections dulled to embrace them, but because human life and human capacity are bounded things; the heart can be devoted but to one object, and the winning of the great prizes of earthly endeavor asks for an intensity of purpose, which in the Christian has found another centre.[56]

Remember.

God's livery is a very plain one; but its wearers have good reason to be content. If it have not so much gold lace about it as Satan's, it keeps out foul weather better, and is besides a great deal cheaper.[12]

Remember,

He who loves with purity considers not the gift of the lover, but the love of the giver.[23]

Remember,

If it be God whom we love in loving one, then shall the bright halo of her spirit expand itself over all existence, till every human face we look upon shall share in its transfiguration, and the old forgotten traces of brotherhood be lit up by it; and our love, instead of pining discomforted, shall be lured upward and

ANGEL VOICES.

Open not thine heart to every man.

upward by low, angelic voices, which recede before it forever, as it mounts from brightening summit on the delectable mountains of aspirations and resolve and deed.[12]

REMEMBER,

While others are curious in the choice of good air, and chiefly solicitous for healthful habitations, study thou conversation, and be critical in thy consortion. The aspects, conjunctions, and configurations of the stars, which mutually diversify, intend, or qualify their influences, are but the varieties of their nearer or farther conversation with one another, and like the consortion of men, whereby they become better or worse, and even exchange their natures.

He who must needs have company, must needs have sometimes bad company. Be able to be alone. Lose not the advantage of solitude, and the society of thyself; nor be only content, but delight to be alone and single with Omnipresency. He who is thus prepared, the day is not uneasy, nor the night black unto him.[18]

REMEMBER,

A good jest, well timed, for misfortune, may

Edify one another.

prove as food and drink,—strength to the arm, digestion to the stomach, courage to the heart. It is better than wisdom or wine. A prosperous man may afford to be melancholy: but if the miserable are so, they are worse than dead,—but it is sure to kill them.[57]

> The heart-gates, mighty, open either way,—
> Come they to feast, or go they forth to pray.[58]

REMEMBER.

Any boy can teach a man, but it takes a man to teach a boy anything.[40]

REMEMBER,

When the great God lets loose a thinker on this planet, then all things are at risk. There is not a piece of science, but its flank may be turned to-morrow; there is not any literary reputation, nor the so-called eternal names of fame, that may not be revised and condemned. . . . . . He claps wings to the sides of all the solid old lumber of the world.[15]

> Yea, copyists shall die, spark out and out;
> Minds which combine and make, alone can tell
> The bearings and the workings of all things
> In and upon each other.[2]

REMEMBER

The gentle words of Meta Klopstock, who

The life of man upon earth is a continual warfare.

said, "Though I love my friends dearly, and though they are good, I have, however, much to pardon, except in the single Klopstock alone. *He* is good, really good,—good in all the foldings of his heart. I know him and *sometimes I think, if we knew others in the same manner, the better we should find them.* For it may be an action displeases us which would please us if we knew its true aim and whole extent.

Remember.

If a man is not rising upwards to be an angel, depend upon it he is sinking downwards to be a devil. He cannot stop at the beast. The most savage of men are not beasts; they are worse, a great deal worse.

As there is much beast and some devil in man, so is there some angel and some God in him. The beast and the devil may be conquered, but, in this life, never wholly destroyed."[19]

> Life is a business, not good cheer
>   Ever in warres.
> The sun still shineth there or here,
>   Whereas the stars
> Watch an advantage to appear.
>
> O that I were an orange-tree,
>   That busie plant!

In your patience possess ye your souls.

> Then should I ever laden be,
>   And never want
> Some fruit for him that dressed me.[70]

> There sits not on the wilderness' edge
>   In the dusk lodges of the wintry North,
> Nor couches in the rice-field's slimy sedge,
>   Nor on the cold, wild waters ventures forth,
> Who waits not, in the pauses of his toil,
>   With hope that spirits in the air may sing;
> Who upward turns not at propitious times,
>   Breathless, his silent features listening,
> In desert and in lodge, on marsh and main,
>   *To feed his hungry heart and conquer pain.*[58]

REMEMBER,

Dear to us are those who love us: the swift moments we spend with them are a compensation for a great deal of misery; they enlarge our life; but dearer are those who reject us as unworthy, for they add another life; they build a heaven before us whereof we had not dreamed, and thereby supply to us new powers out of the recesses of the spirit, and urge us to new and unattempted performances.[16]

REMEMBER,

There are "eternal homes, built deep in poor men's hearts," for such as do God's work on earth.[63]

Charity never faileth.

Remember,

So to regard the absent who are out of hearing as virtually under the protection of that law of Jewish charity, —

"Thou shalt not curse the deaf." [64]

Remember,

That love never contracts its circles: they widen by as fixed and sure a law as those around a pebble cast into still water. The angel of love, when, full of sorrow, he followed the first exiles, behind whom the gates of Paradise shut with that mournful clang, (of which some faint echo has lingered in the hearts of all their offspring,) unwittingly snapped off and brought away in his hand the seed-pod of one of the never-failing flowers which grew there. Into all dreary and desolate places fell some of its blessed kernels; they asked but little soil to root themselves in, and in this narrow patch of our poor clay they sprang most quickly and sturdily. Gladly they grew, and from them all time has been sown with whatever gives a higher hope to the soul, or makes life nobler and more god-like; while from the over-arching sky of poesy sweet dew forever falls, to nurse and

Charity suffereth long, and envieth not.

keep them green and fresh from the world's dust.[12]

Like bird to sunshine fled he to a smile.[66]

REMEMBER,

If he loves me, the merit is not mine, the fault will be if he ceases.[65]

REMEMBER,

It was not by retiring into himself, but by going out of himself, that CHRIST OVERCAME THE WORLD; not by spiritual pathology and self-torture, but by veritable "sufferings," that he "became perfect"; not by measuring his own emotions, but by oblivion of them amid a crowd of toils, a succession of fulfilled resolves, a profuse expenditure of life and effort having others for their object, that he rose above the dignity of men, and ripened the divinest spirit for the skies.[80]

REMEMBER,

There is "woe to the nation or the society in which the individualizing and separating process is going on in the human mind! Whether it take the form of a religion or of a philosophy, it is at once the sign and cause of senility, decay, and death. If a man begins

Bear ye one another's burdens.

to forget he is a social being, a member of a body, and that the only truths which are worthy objects of his philosophical search are those which are equally true for every man, which will equally avail every man, which he must proclaim as far as he can to every man, from the proudest sage to the meanest outcast,— he enters, I believe, into a lie, and helps forward the dissolution of that society of which he is a member. I care little whether what he holds be true or not. If it be true, he has made it a lie by appropriating it proudly and selfishly to himself, and by excluding others from it. He has darkened his own power of vision by that act of self-appropriation, so that, even if he sees a truth, he can see it only refractedly, discolored, by the medium of his own private likes and dislikes, and fulfil that great and truly philosophic law, that he who loveth not his brother is in darkness, and knoweth not whither he goeth.[43]

Remember.

All good conversation, manners, and action come from a spontaneity which forgets usages and makes the moment great.[16]

Out of the heart are the issues of life.

> Action is transitory, — a step, a blow,
> The motion of a muscle — this way or that —
> 'T is done. . . . . .
> Suffering is permanent, obscure and dark,
> And has the nature of infinity.[85]

Remember.

Our contentments stand upon the tops of pyramids, ready to fall off, and the insecurity of their enjoyments abrupteth our tranquillities. To enjoy true happiness, we must travel into a very far country, and even out of ourselves; for the pearl we seek for is not to be found in the Indian, but in the empyrean ocean.[18]

Remember.

Prayer is a constant source of invigoration to self-discipline; not the thoughtless praying which is a thing of custom, but that which is sincere, earnest, watchful. Let a man ask himself whether he really would have the thing he prays for; let him think, while he is praying for a spirit of forgiveness, whether, even at that moment, he is disposed to give up the luxury of anger. If not, what a horrible mockery it is.[49]

Remember

To make thy door fast behind thee, and invite Jesus, thy beloved, to come unto thee,

Commune with thy heart and be still.

and enlighten thy darkness with his light. Abide faithfully with him in this retirement, for thou canst not find so much peace in any other place."[21]

Thus shalt thou make "thine eyes the homes of silent prayer."[4]

Remember.

No man can safely go abroad who does not love to stay at home.[23]

Said Walter Scott, I have been always careful to place my mind in the most tranquil posture which it can assume during my private exercises of devotion.

Be not sorry that men do not know you, but be sorry that you are ignorant of men.[67]

Remember.

"There is a hush in our nation's heart. An expectancy, a waiting and longing for some unspoken word, which sometimes seems awful in the bounty of its promise. I know men educated to speak, with the burden of a speaker's vocation on their hearts, but now these many years remaining heroically silent; the fountains of a fresh consciousness sweet within them, but not yet flowing into speech, and they too earnest, too expectant, too sure of the future, to say aught beneath the strain.

Thy speech bewrayeth thee.

'Why do you not speak?' was inquired of one. 'Because I can keep silent,' he said. 'And the word I am to utter will command me.'"

REMEMBER,

Wouldst thou see thine insufficiency more plainly, view thyself at thy devotions; to what end was religion instituted, but to teach thee thine infirmities? to remind thee of thy weakness? to show thee, that from Heaven alone thou art to hope for good?[68]

REMEMBER,

In all thy life's course, that Truth is strong next to the Almighty; she needs no policies, no stratagems, no licensings, to make her victorious! Though all the winds of doctrine were let loose to play upon the earth, so Truth be in the field, we injure her to misdoubt her strength. Let Truth and Falsehood grapple: who ever knew Truth put to the worse in a free and open encounter?[17]

> Truth, crushed to earth, shall rise again;
> The eternal years of God are hers;
> While Error, wounded, writhes in pain,
> And dies amidst her worshippers.[85]

REMEMBER,

A word spoken in season, at the right moment, is the mother of ages.[56]

We were foolish, living in malice and envy.

Let it be said of thee, —

"Words of good cheer were most native to her lips."

Remember,

Reserve is the truest expression of respect towards those who are its objects.[59]

Remember,

It is not always the dark place that hinders, but sometimes the dim eye.[64]

> 'T is by comparison an easy task
> Earth to despise; but to converse with heaven, —
> This is not easy.[b]

> Know,
> Without or star or angel for their guide,
> Who worship God shall find him. Humble love,
> And not proud reason, keeps the door of heaven.
> Love finds admission where proud science fails.[61]

Remember,

Augustine calls *envy* the besetting sin of the Devil, who envied Jehovah in heaven, and Adam in paradise, and the essence of whose torment is a thought of happiness which he cannot share. To an envious soul true joy is impossible; — if perfect in conditions of manhood, it will writhe at the thought of angelic spheres and pinions; if raised to Gabriel's ministry in the very presence of God, it will

Let us walk honestly, not in strife and envying.

be in anguish at the sight of that higher throne and the loftier One that sitteth on it.[70]

Wisdom consists in being very humble, as if we were incapable of anything, yet ardent, as if we could do all.[67]

Remember,

Since the stars of heaven do differ in glory; since it hath pleased the Almighty hand to honor the north pole with lights above the south; since there are some stars so bright that they can hardly be looked upon, some so dim that they can scarcely be seen, and vast numbers not to be seen at all even by artificial eyes; read thou the earth in heaven, and things below from above. Look contentedly upon the scattered difference of things, and expect not equality in lustre, dignity, or perfection in regions or persons below; where numerous numbers must be content to stand like lacteous or nebulous stars, little taken notice of, or dim in their generations. All which may be contentedly allowable in the affairs and ends of this world, and in suspension unto what will be in the order of things hereafter, and the new system of mankind which will be in the world to come; when the

I ascend unto my Father and your Father.

last may be the first, and the first the last; when Lazarus may sit above Cæsar, and the just obscure on earth shall shine like the sun in heaven; when personations shall cease, and histrionism of happiness be over; when reality shall rule, and all shall be as they shall be forever.[18]

Remember.

The world is not so framed that it can keep quiet. Could we perfect human nature, we might expect perfection everywhere; but as it is, there will always be this wavering hither and thither; one part must suffer while the other is at ease. Envy and egotism will be always at work like bad demons, and party conflicts (and those of sects) find no end. Do what you were born or have learned to do, and avoid hindering others from doing the same.

> Trace the forms
> Of atoms moving with incessant change
> Their elemental round; behold the seeds
> Of being, and the energy of life
> Kindling the mass with ever-active flame;
> Then to the secrets of the working mind
> Attentive turn.[51]

Remember.

A judicious silence is always better than truth spoken without charity.

Abundance of idleness was in her and in her daughters.

Remember.

The idle are

> "Like ships that sailed for sunny isles,
> But never came to shore."

Remember.

What wonders lie in every day,—had we the sight, as happily we have not, to decipher it: for is not every meanest day the conflux of two eternities?[36]

She was mistaken in saying bad authors may amuse our idleness. Leontion knows not, then, how sweet and sacred idleness is.[65]

Remember.

It is no more possible for an idle man to keep together a certain stock of knowledge, than it is possible to keep together a stock of ice exposed to the meridian sun. Every day destroys a fact, a relation, or an influence; and the only method of preserving the bulk and value of the pile is by constantly adding to it.

> Ydelnes, that is the gate of all harmes.
> An ydil man is like an hous that hath
> Noone walls;
> The develes may enter on every side.[44]

Weep with them that weep.

Indolence is, methinks, says Steele, an intermediate state between pleasure and pain, and very much unbecoming any part of our life after we are out of the nurse's arms.

REMEMBER,

After his blood, that which a man can next give out of himself is a tear.[91]

REMEMBER,

The mercy of God hath singled out but few to be the signals of his justice, leaving the generality of mankind to the pedagogy of example.[18]

Do not trials and sorrows (also, it is true, deep joys) shared between two friends, partings, dangers, above all, the having stood together in the presence of death, deepen the channel of our affection in deepening that of our existence? Are not such moments as it were sacramental, bringing us nearer each other in bringing us nearer God, from whom the poor unrealities of time, *unworthy of us as they are of Him*, too much divide us? When the veil of the temple, even this poor worn garment of our humanity, is rent from the top to the bottom, we catch glimpses of the inner glory. "They who love," as says St. Chrysostom, "if it be but man, not God,"

Passing the time of thy sojourning in holy fear.

will know what I mean, when I speak of joys springing out of the very heart of anguish, and holding to it by a common and inseparable life; will understand how it comes that the pale flowers which thrust themselves out of the ruins of hope, of endeavor, of affection, yes, even out of the mournful wreck of intellect itself, should breathe out a deep and intimate fragrance, such as the broad wealth of air and sunshine never yet gave.[56]

Constantly endeavor to do the will of another rather than thine own:

Constantly choose rather to want less, than to have more:

Constantly choose the lowest place, and to be humble to all:

Constantly desire and pray that the will of God may be perfectly accomplished in thee, and concerning thee.

Verily, I say unto thee, he that doeth this enters into the region of rest and peace.[23]

Remember.

That though there is something painful, yea, terrific, in feeling one's self involved in the great wheel of society, which goes whirling on, crushing thousands at every turn, yet though

I will purely purge away thy dross.

this relation of the individual to the mass is the sternest and most frightful of all conflicts between necessity and free will, here too conflict *should* be harmony, and *will* be so. Put, then, far away from thy soul all desire of retaliation, all angry thoughts, all disposition to overcome or humiliate an adversary, and be assured thou hast done much to abolish gallows, chains, and prisons, though thou hast never written or spoken a word on the criminal code.

> 'T is Nature's law,
> That none, the meanest of created things,
> Of forms created the most vile and brute,
> The dullest or most noxious, should exist
> Divorced from good, — a spirit and pulse of good,
> A life and soul, to every mode of being
> Inseparably linked. Then be assured
> That least of all can aught — that ever owned
> The heaven-regarding eye and front sublime,
> Which man is born to — sink, howe'er depressed,
> So low as to be scorned without a sin,
> Without offence to God, cast out of view.[35]

REMEMBER.

The web of our life is of a mingled yarn, good and ill together; our virtues would be proud, if our faults whipped them not; and our crimes would despair, if they were not cherished by our virtues.[50]

Be content with such things as ye have.

Remember,

Every moment instructs, and every object; for wisdom is infused into every form. It has been poured into us as blood; it convulsed us as pain; it slid into us as pleasure; it enveloped us in dull, melancholy days, or in days of cheerful labor: we did not guess its essence until after long time.[15]

Remember,

And repine not over your daily lot; but regard all your labor solely as a symbol; at bottom, it does not signify whether we make pots or dishes.[8]

"The reward of work well done, is the having done it."

> Teach us for all joys to crave
> Benediction, pure and high,
> Own them given, endure them gone,
> Shrink from their hardening touch, yet prize them won;
> Prize them as rich odors, meet
> For Love to lavish on His sacred feet;
> Prize them as sparkles bright
> Of heavenly dew, from yon o'erflowing well of light.[1]

Remember,

Happy the man who can embark his small adventure of deeds and thoughts upon the shallow waters round his own home, or send

The kingdom of God is within you.

them afloat on the wide sea of humanity, with no great anxiety in either case as to what reception they may meet with.[58]

All the glory and beauty of Christ are manifested within, and there he delights to dwell; his visits there are frequent, his condescension amazing, his conversation sweet, his comforts refreshing; and the peace that he brings passeth all understanding.[21]

> Yet much remains
> To conquer still; peace hath her victories
> No less renowned than war.[17]

Remember.

And make search for that "inmost centre in us all, where truth abides in fulness"; and there learn that to *know*

> Rather consists in opening out a way
> Whence the imprisoned splendor may dart forth,
> Than in effecting entry for a light
> Supposed to be without.[14]

Remember.

The first creature of God in the works of the days was the light of the sense; the last was the light of reason; and his Sabbath work ever since is the illumination of his Spirit.[37]

Yet forget not that "the whole world is a phylactery, and everything we see an item of the wisdom, power, or goodness of God."[13]

Be content with such things as ye have.

REMEMBER,

Every moment instructs, and every object; for wisdom is infused into every form. It has been poured into us as blood; it convulsed us as pain; it slid into us as pleasure; it enveloped us in dull, melancholy days, or in days of cheerful labor: we did not guess its essence until after long time.[15]

REMEMBER,

And repine not over your daily lot; but regard all your labor solely as a symbol; at bottom, it does not signify whether we make pots or dishes.[9]

"The reward of work well done, is the having done it."

> Teach us for all joys to crave
> Benediction, pure and high, .
> Own them given, endure them gone,
> Shrink from their hardening touch, yet prize them won;
> Prize them as rich odors, meet
> For Love to lavish on His sacred feet;
> Prize them as sparkles bright
> Of heavenly dew, from yon o'erflowing well of light.[1]

REMEMBER,

Happy the man who can embark his small adventure of deeds and thoughts upon the shallow waters round his own home, or send

The kingdom of God is within you.

them afloat on the wide sea of humanity, with no great anxiety in either case as to what reception they may meet with.[58]

All the glory and beauty of Christ are manifested within, and there he delights to dwell; his visits there are frequent, his condescension amazing, his conversation sweet, his comforts refreshing; and the peace that he brings passeth all understanding.[21]

> Yet much remains
> To conquer still; peace hath her victories
> No less renowned than war.[17]

REMEMBER.

And make search for that "inmost centre in us all, where truth abides in fulness"; and there learn that to *know*

> Rather consists in opening out a way
> Whence the imprisoned splendor may dart forth,
> Than in effecting entry for a light
> Supposed to be without.[14]

REMEMBER.

The first creature of God in the works of the days was the light of the sense; the last was the light of reason; and his Sabbath work ever since is the illumination of his Spirit.[37]

Yet forget not that "the whole world is a phylactery, and everything we see an item of the wisdom, power, or goodness of God."[18]

If so be that we suffer with him,

Remember,

Man is buried in consecrated earth;—even thus should we bury great and rare occurrences in a beautiful tomb of remembrance, to which each one may approach and celebrate the memory thereof.

Said Margaret Fuller: "All the good I have ever done has been by calling on every nature for its highest. I will admit that sometimes I have been wanting in gentleness, but never in tenderness or in noble faith."

Remember,

To run not too hotly in the pursuit of earthly knowledge, which is, after all, but "broken wonder."

Remember,

Nature, indeed, draws tears out of the eyes, and sighs out of the breast, so quickly, that the wise man can never wholly lay aside the garb of mourning from his body; but let his soul wear none. Though philosophy may not, like a stroke of the brush of Rubens, transform a laughing child into a weeping one, it is well if it change the full mourning of the soul into half-mourning, by teaching us how to bear present transient ills.

We may be also glorified together.

Even physical pain shoots its sparks upon us out of the electrical condenser of the imagination. The most acute pangs could be endured calmly, if they lasted only the sixtieth part of a second ; but, in fact, we never have to endure an hour of pain, but only a succession of the sixtieth parts of a second, the sixty beams of which are collected into the burning focus of a second, and directed upon our nerves by the imagination alone. The most painful part of our bodily pain is that which is bodiless, or immaterial, namely, our impatience, and the delusion that it will last forever.[34]

REMEMBER.

Firmian did well in that he touched lightly and passed hastily in narration over the bad year of his stomach, over his *hard times*, over the figurative winter of his life, though, in the eyes of his intimate friend, his pallid, withered face, and his sunken eye, formed the frontispiece of his months of ice, and was a winter landscape of this snow-covered portion of his path of life; because no one deserves the name of *man* who makes a greater fuss about the wounds of poverty than a girl makes about those of her ears, since, equally in both cases, hooks, whereby to suspend jewels, are inserted into the wounds.⁵⁴

> Light came from darkness, gladness from despair,
> As, when the sunlight fadeth from the earth,
> Star after star comes out upon the sky,
> And shining worlds, that had not been revealed
> In day's full light, are then made manifest.
> Thus it is when, light of earth shut out,
> Our thoughts turned inward, we discover there
> Things of immortal wonder, living springs
> Of an unfailing comfort; hidden things
> Brighter than earth's allurements. We can trace
> The operations of the immortal mind,
> On its high path to excellence and joy,
> And see the prize of its high calling there.⁷³

Goethe says: "Perhaps we shall be blessed (hereafter) with what here on earth has been denied us, to know one another merely by seeing one another, and thence more thoroughly to love one another."

Remember.

And judge not man by his outward manifestation of faith; for some there are, who tremblingly reach out shaking hands to the guidance of Faith; others, who stoutly venture in the dark their human confidence, their leader, which they mistake for Faith; some, whose Hope totters upon crutches; others,

When I am weak, then am I strong.

who stalk into futurity upon stilts. The difference is chiefly constitutional with them.[74]

> Each is but
> An infant crying in the night,
> And with no language but a cry.[4]

REMEMBER,

The more consciousness in our thoughts and words, and the less in our impulses and general actions, the better and more healthful the state both of head and heart. As the flowers from an orange-tree in its time of blossoming, that bourgeon forth, expand, fall, and are momently replaced, such is the sequence of hourly and momently charities in a pure and gracious soul. The modern fiction which depictures the son of Cytherea with a bandage round his eyes, is not without a spiritual meaning. There is a sweet and holy blindness in Christian love, even as there is a blindness of life, yea, and of genius too, in the moment of productive energy.[18]

REMEMBER,

In thy silent wishing, thy voiceless, uttered prayer, let the desire be not cherished that afflictions may not visit thee; for well has it been said, —

Glory in tribulation.

Such prayers never seem to have wings."

Extremity is the trier of spirits;
Common chances common men could bear: —
When the sea is calm, all boats alike
Show mastership in floating.⁵⁰

"If my bark sink, 't is to another sea."

REMEMBER.

Pain is the deepest thing we have in our nature, and union through pain has always seemed more real and holy than any other.⁷⁵

REMEMBER.

Rabia, a devout Arabian woman, who being asked in her last illness how she endured the extremity of her sufferings, made answer, "They who look upon God's face do not feel his hand."⁷⁷

REMEMBER.

In no life does the secret of all tragedy, the conflict between the will and circumstance, so unfold itself as in that of the Christian; he, of all men, feels and mourns over that sharp, ever-recurring contrast of our existence, — the glorious capabilities, the limited attainments of man's nature and destiny below...... If he would stretch forth his hand and live by what he can reach of absolute truth, he will

Put on the whole armor of God.

quickly come across the flaming sword turning *every way* to keep the way of the Tree of Life.[56]

REMEMBER,

Interior freedom and exterior necessity, these are the two poles of the Tragic World.[73]

REMEMBER,

A straight line is the shortest in morals as well as in geometry.[9]

Be thou not

a rogue in grain,
Veneered with sanctimonious theory.[4]

REMEMBER,

If men lived like men indeed, their houses would be temples.[81]

REMEMBER,

The great secret both of health and successful industry is the absolute yielding up of one's consciousness to the business and diversion of the hour, — never permitting the one to infringe in the least degree upon the other.[42]

REMEMBER,

What is human life, if not a vast desire and a great attempt?

What profiteth it a man if he gain

REMEMBER,

To rest not in an ovation, but a triumph over thy passions. Let anger walk hanging down the head; let malice go manacled, and envy fettered, after thee. Behold within thee the long train of thy trophies, not without thee. Make the quarrelling Lapithyles sleep, and Centaurs within lie quiet. Chain up the unruly legion of thy breast. Lead thine own captivity captive, and be Cæsar within thyself.[18]

REMEMBER,

'T is
> the hypocrites that ope Heaven's door
> Obsequious to the sinful man of riches,—
> But put the wicked, naked, barelegged poor
> In parish stocks instead of breeches.[62]

REMEMBER,

The capital art of life is to renew and augment your power by its expenditure. It was intimated some eighteen centuries since, that the highest are obtained only by loss of the same; and the transmutation of loss into gain is the essence and perfection of all spiritual economics. Now of this art of arts he is already master who steadily draws upon his own spiritual resources. The soul is an ex-

the whole world and lose his own soul?

traordinary well; the way to replenish is to draw from it.[13]

Remember,

It is a poor centre of a man's actions, himself. It is right earth. For that only stands fast upon her own centre, whereas all things that have affinity with the heavens move upon the centre of another, which they benefit.

Wisdom for a man's self is, in many branches thereof, a depraved thing. It is the wisdom of rats, that will be sure to leave a house somewhat before it fall. It is the wisdom of the fox, that thrusts out the badger who digged and made room for him. It is the wisdom of crocodiles, that shed tears when they would devour. . . . . . And when they have all their time sacrificed to themselves, they become in the end themselves sacrifices to the inconstancy of fortune, whose wings they thought by their self-wisdom to have pinioned.[55]

Remember,

Man is greater than a world, — than systems of worlds; there is more mystery in the union of soul with the physical, than in the creation of a universe.[84]

What shall a man give in exchange for his soul?

I never could feel any force in the arguments for a plurality of worlds, in the common acceptation of that term. The vulgar inference is *in alio genere* (for other beings). What in the eye of an intellectual and omnipotent Being is the whole sidereal system to the soul of one man for whom Christ died?[10]

I will make a man more precious than fine gold; even a man than the golden wedge of Ophir. — Isa. xiii. 12.

Coleridge adds: "A lady once asked me, 'What then could be the intention in creating so many great bodies, so apparently useless to us?' I said, I did not know, except, perhaps, to make *dirt* cheap!"

REMEMBER,
Things are of the snake.[15]

To commiserate is sometimes more than to give; for money is external to a man's self, but he who bestows compassion communicates his own soul.[86]

"There's naught so fathomless as woe unshared."

We have our younger brothers, too,
The poor, the outcast, and the trodden down,
Left fatherless on earth to pine for bread;
They are a-hungered for our love and care,

He who giveth to the poor, lendeth to the Lord.

It is their spirits that are famishing,
And our dear Father, in his Testament,
Bequeathed them to us as our dearest trust,
Wherefore we shall give a straight account.
Woe, if we have forgotten them, and left
Those souls that might have grown so fair and glad,
That only wanted a kind word from us,
To be so free and gently beautiful, —
Left them to feel their birthright a curse,
To grow all lean, and cramped, and full of sores,
And — last, sad change, that surely comes to all
Shut out from manhood by their brother man —
To turn mere wolves for lack of aught to love.[12]

Shall we speak of the inspiration of a poet or a priest, and not of the heart impelled by love and self-devotion to the lowliest work in the lowliest way of life?[87]

REMEMBER.

Among those whom the world calls poor, there is less vital force, a lower tone of life, more ill-health, more weakness, more early death. There are also less self-respect, ambition, and hope, than among the independent.[84]

REMEMBER,

He who knows, like St. Paul, both how to spare and how to abound, has great knowledge; for if we take account of all the virtues with which money is mixed up, — hon-

If ye know these things, happy are ye if ye do them.

esty, justice, generosity, charity, frugality, forethought, self-sacrifice, — and of their correlative vices, it is a knowledge which goes near to cover the length and breadth of humanity; and a right measure and manner in getting, saving, spending, giving, taking, lending, borrowing, and bequeathing would almost argue a perfect man.[89]

Felicity is nothing else than the use of virtue in prosperity.[95]

REMEMBER,

He that believes only what he understands, has the shortest known creed.[96]

> God judgeth us by what we know of right,
> Rather than what we practise that is wrong
> Unknowingly.[12]

REMEMBER,

In your intercourse with sects, — The sublime and abstruse doctrines of Christian *belief* belong to the Church; but the *faith* of the individual, centred in his heart, is, or may be, collateral to them. Faith is subjective.[19]

> Whom the heart of man shuts out,
> Straightway the heart of God takes in.[12]

Thou wilt not leave my soul in hell.

Remember.

The necessary mansions of our restored selves are those two contrary and incompatible places we call Heaven and Hell; to define them, or strictly to determine what and where these are, surpasseth my divinity. That elegant Apostle, which seemed to have a glimpse of heaven, hath left but a negative description thereof.[18]

I have so fixed my contemplations on heaven, that I have almost forgot the idea of hell, and am afraid rather to lose the joys of the one than endure the misery of the other; to be deprived of them is a perfect hell, and needs, methinks, no addition to complete our afflictions.[18]

> Know ye, there are two worlds of life and death;
> One, that which thou beholdest; but the other
> Is underneath the grave, where do inhabit
> The shadows of all forms that think and live,
> Till death *unite* them, and they part no more.[97]

Remember.

They who are incapable of self-devouring emotion and brooding melancholy may easily find in rules of duty a safeguard against any such wrong-doing as would produce consequences very painful to them; but a fervid and meditative spirit carries conscience with

Ye cannot serve God and Mammon.

it as a divine curse, if this be not transfigured and glorified into the revelation of a good higher than all laws of duty.[98]

> O tell her, brief is life, but love is long,
> And brief the sun of summer in the North,
> And brief the moon of beauty in the South.[4]

REMEMBER,

A weak mind sinks under prosperity, as well as under adversity. A strong and deep one has two highest tides, — when the moon is at the full, and when there is no moon.[99]

REMEMBER,

And lay on thy heart the deep meaning of these words : —

> "Exceeding fair she was not, and yet fair
> In that she never studied to be fairer
> Than Nature meant her; beauty cost her nothing."[100]

REMEMBER,

The conflict of Christianity is the harder because it is civil; it has allied itself with that against which it must contend to the death, or be itself overcome of it. Hence its fierce collisions, its sorrowful victories; hence too its still more sad, more fatal compromises, its unholy, unhallowing alliances, "the Woman sitting upon the Beast," — the compact between

Give to him that asketh.

the Church and the World, at the sight of which he who had learned so many secrets from his beloved Master yet "wondered with great admiration."[50]

Remember,

To be charitable before wealth make thee covetous, and lose not the glory of the mite. If riches increase, let thy mind hold pace with them; and think it not enough to be liberal, but munificent. Though a cup of cold water from some hand may not be without its reward, yet stick not thou for wine and oil for the wounds of the distressed; and treat the poor, as our Saviour did the multitude, to the relics of some baskets. Diffuse thy beneficence early, and while thy treasures call thee master; there may be an Atropos of thy fortunes before that of thy life, and thy wealth cut off before that hour when all men shall be poor; for the justice of death looks equally upon the dead, and Charon expects no more from Alexander than from Irus.[19]

> Heaven doth with us as we with torches do, —
> Not light them for themselves; for if our virtues
> Did not go forth of us, 't were all alike
> As if we had them not.[50]

The world hateth you.

REMEMBER the words of Archdeacon Hare: There are persons who, by a certain felicity of nature, through a peculiar combination of magnanimity and generosity with gentleness and open-hearted frankness, loving to give the very best of what they have, are gifted with a sort of divining-rod for drawing out what is hidden in the hearts of their brethren; and of such persons I have known no finer example than Sterling. For in him, as in such persons it must ever be, the nobleness of his outward look and gesture and manner betokened that of his spirit, and showed that the whole man, heart and soul and mind, was uttering himself in his eloquent speech.

> O, if there is one law above the rest
> Written in wisdom, — if there is a word
> That I would trace as with a pen of fire
> Upon the unsunned temper of a child, —
> If there is anything that keeps the mind
> Open to angel visits, and repels
> The ministry of ill, — 't is human love!
> God has made nothing worthy of contempt.
> The smallest pebble in the well of truth
> Has its peculiar meaning, and will stand
> When man's best monuments have passed away.
> The law of Heaven is *love*, and though its name
> Has been usurped by passion, and profaned
> To its unholy uses through all time,
> Still the eternal principle is pure;

Be not forgetful to entertain strangers.

And in these deep affections that we feel
Omnipotent within us, we but see
The lavish measure in which love is given,
And in the yearning tenderness of a child
For every bird that sings above his head,
And every creature feeding on the hills,
And every tree and flower and running brook,
We see how everything was MADE TO LOVE,
And how they err who, in a world like this,
Find anything to hate but human pride![66]

REMEMBER,

Hospitality is threefold: for one's family, this is of necessity; for strangers, this is courtesy; for the poor, this is charity.

Measure not thy entertainment of a guest by his estate, but thine own. Because he is a lord, forget not thou art but a gentleman; otherwise, if with feasting him thou breakest thyself, he will not cure thy rupture, and perchance rather deride than pity thee.

Company is one of the greatest pleasures of the nature of man. For the beams of joy are made hotter by reflection, when related to another; and otherwise gladness itself must grieve for want of one to express itself to.[67]

Be merry, man, and take not sair to mind
The wavering of this wretched world of sorrow;
To God be humble, to thy friend be kind,

Thereby some have entertained angels unawares.

And with thy neighbors gladly lend and borrow;
His chance to-night, it may be thine to-morrow.

. . . . .

Be charitable and humble in thine estate,
   For warldly honor lastes but a day.
   For trouble in earth take no melancholy;
Be rich in patience, if thou in gudes be poor;
   Who lives merrily, he lives mightely:
Without sadness avails no treasure.[101]

Remember,

In how many instances servants, living under the same roof with us, share none of our feelings nor we of theirs; their presence is felt as a restraint; we know nothing about them but that they perform certain set duties; and, in short, they may be said to be a kind of live furniture. There is something very repugnant to Christianity in all this. Surely there might be much more sympathy between masters and servants without endangering the good part of our social system. At any rate, we may be certain that a fastidious reserve towards our fellow-creatures is not the way in which true dignity or strength of mind will ever manifest themselves in us.[49]

   For each enclosed spirit is a star
     Enlightening his own little sphere,
   Whose light, though fetch and borrowed from far,
     Both mornings makes and evenings there.[54]

The trying of your faith worketh patience.

REMEMBER.

Faith provides for every affection, every want and aspiration. It stretches itself over humanity as the prophet stretched himself above the child,—eye to eye, mouth to mouth, heart to heart ; and to work a kindred miracle, to bring back life to the dead, by restoring the *One* to the One, — *the whole nature of Man to the whole nature of God.*[56]

REMEMBER,

The fluctuations to which spiritual life is subject show the wisdom and goodness of God in making so much of it to reside in duty, *a principle independent of the variations of feeling*. There are long seasons of banishment from God's presence, unconnected, perhaps, with any sense of his displeasure, in which the soul must say, "Make me as one of thy hired servants."[56]

> Sense of pleasure
> We may well spare out of life, and live content ;
> Which is the happiest life.[17]

REMEMBER.

There is no real elevation of mind in contempt of little things ; it is, on the contrary, from too narrow views that we consider those things of little importance which have in fact

Be ye angry and sin not.

such extensive consequences. The more apt we are to neglect small things, the more we ought to fear the effects of this negligence, be watchful over ourselves, and place around us, if possible, some insurmountable barrier to this remissness.[59]

> Patience! Why, 't is the soul of peace:
> Of all the virtues, 't is nearest kin to heaven.
> It makes men look like gods. The best of men
> That e'er wore earth about him was a sufferer, —
> A soft, meek, patient, humble, tranquil spirit;
> The first true gentleman that ever breathed.[102]

REMEMBER,

Anger is one of the sinews of the soul; he that wants it hath a maimed mind, and with Jacob, sinew-shrunk in the hollow of his thigh, must needs halt. Nor is it good to converse with such as cannot be angry, and with the Caspian Sea never ebb nor flow.[40]

> To climb steep hills
> Requires slow pace at first: anger is like
> A full hot horse, who, being allowed his way,
> Self-mettle tires him.[50]

REMEMBER.

If it be pain to us to love, and at the same time to contradict, to refuse with the head what the heart grants, it is all the sweeter to us to find ourselves and our faith transplanted

Let not the sun go down upon your wrath.

forwards in a younger being. Life is then a beautiful night, in which not one star goes down but another rises in its place.[34]

"And he answered them nothing."

O mighty Nothing! unto thee,
Nothing, we owe all things that be.
God spake once, when he all things made,
He saved all, when he Nothing said.[103]

REMEMBER,

That such an anger alone is criminal which is against charity to myself or my neighbor; but anger against sin is a holy zeal, and an effect of love to God and my brother, for whose interest I am passionate, like a concerned person. And if I take care that my anger makes no reflection of scorn or cruelty upon the offender, or of pride and violence, or transportation to myself, anger becomes charity and duty. And when one commended Charilaus, the king of Sparta, for a gentle, a good, and a meek prince, his colleague said well, "How can he be good, who is not an enemy even to vicious persons?"[20]

REMEMBER,

Quiet gives not a strength to human kind,
To leave all suffering powerless at its feet,

My peace I give unto you.

> But keeps within the temple of the mind
> A golden altar, and a mercy-seat:
>   A spiritual ark,
>   Bearing the peace of God
>   Above the waters dark,
>   And o'er the desert's sod.
> How beautiful within our souls to keep
> This treasure, the All-Merciful hath given;
> To feel, when we awake, and when we sleep,
> Its incense round us, like a breeze from heaven!
>   Quiet at hearth and home,
>   Where the heart's joys begin;
>   Quiet where'er we roam,
>   Quiet around, within.[105]

Hooker's anger is said to have been like a vial of clear water, which, when shook, beads at the top, but instantly subsides, without any soil or sediment of uncharitableness.

REMEMBER.

Recreation is a second creation, when business hath almost annihilated one's spirits. It is the breathing of the soul, which otherwise would be stifled with continual business.[40]

As a countenance is made beautiful by the soul's shining through it, so the world is beautiful by the shining through it of a God.[104]

REMEMBER.

The only way for a rich man to be healthy

Your body is the temple.

is, by exercise and abstinence, to live so as if he were poor.[106]

REMEMBER,

There is no temperament which may not be formed to a Christian temper.[107]

Every man is the builder of a temple, called his body, to the god he worships, after a style purely his own; nor can he get off by hammering marble instead. We are all sculptors and painters, and our material is our own flesh and blood and bones. Any nobleness begins at once to refine a man's features, any meanness or sensuality to imbrute them.[108]

REMEMBER.

Life is too short to get over a bad manner; besides, manners are the shadows of virtue.[109]

REMEMBER,

Spill not the morning (the quintessence of the day) in recreations. For sleep itself is a recreation; add not, therefore, sauce to sauce.[40]

REMEMBER.

A man's own observation, what he finds good of, and what he finds hurt of, is the best physic to preserve health. . . . . . To be free-

A show of wisdom in neglecting of the body.

minded, and cheerfully disposed, at hours of meat, and of sleep, and of exercise, is one of the best precepts of long lasting......

Use fasting and full eating, but rather full eating; watching and sleep, but rather sleep; sitting and exercise, but rather exercise; and the like. So shall nature be cherished, and yet taught masteries.[65]

REMEMBER,

Health is the ground which great persons cultivate, whereby they exchange the light flying hours into golden usage. To them it is industry represented in its power; the human riches of time. The minute-glass runs willingly sand of centuries when great ideas are in the healthful moments.[110]

Said Milton: "My morning haunts are, where they should be, at home; not sleeping, nor concocting the surfeits of an irregular feast, but up and stirring; in winter, often ere the sound of any bell awake men to labor or to devotion; in summer, as oft with the bird that first rises, or not much tardier, to read good authors, or cause them to be read till the attention be weary, or memory have its full freight."

He giveth his beloved sleep.

Health and strength are the virtue of the body.[111]

REMEMBER,

We term sleep a death; and yet it is waking that kills us, and destroys those spirits that are the home of life. 'T is indeed a part of life that best expresseth death; for every man truly lives, so long as he acts his nature, or some way makes good the faculties of himself. Themistocles, therefore, that slew his soldier in his sleep, was a merciful executioner; 't is a kind of punishment the mildness of no laws hath invented. I wonder the fancy of Lucan and Seneca did not discover it. It is that death by which we may be literally said to die daily; a death which Adam died before his mortality; a death whereby we live a middle and moderating point between life and death; in fine, so like death, I dare not trust it without my prayers, and an half adieu unto the world, and take my farewell in a colloquy with God.

Virtuous thoughts of the day lay up good treasures for the night; whereby the impressions of imaginary forms arise into softer similitudes, acceptable unto our slumbering selves, and preparatory unto divine impressions. Hereby Solomon's sleep was happy. Thus prepared, Jacob might well dream of angels, on a pillow of stone.[18]

Sadi said, "God gives sleep to the bad, in order that the good may be undisturbed."

> O magic sleep ! O comfortable bird,
> That broodest o'er the troubled sea of the mind,
> Till it is hushed and smooth ! O unconfined
> Restraint ! imprisoned liberty ! great key
> To golden palaces, strange minstrelsy,
> Fountains grotesque, new trees, bespangled caves,
> Echoing grottoes full of tumbling waves,
> And moonlight: ay, to all the mazy world
> Of silvery enchantment ! who, upfurled
> Beneath thy drowsy wing a triple hour,
> But renovates and lives ?[38]

Labor is the Lethe of the Past and of the Present.[34]

Remember.

In the morning, when you awake, accustom yourself to think first upon God, or something in order to his service; and at night also let him close thine eyes, and let your sleep be necessary and healthful, not idle and expensive of time, beyond the needs and conveniences of nature; and sometimes be curious to see the preparation which the sun makes,

The night cometh when no man can work.

when he is coming forth from the chambers of the east.[20]

Remember,

As much as may be to cut off all impertinent and useless employments of your life, unnecessary and fantastic visits, long waitings upon great personages, where neither duty nor necessity nor charity obliges us; all vain meetings, all laborious trifles, and whatsoever spends much time to no real civil, religious, or charitable purpose.

Let not your recreations be lavish spenders of your time, but choose such which are healthful, short, transient, recreative, and apt to refresh you; but at no hand dwell upon them, or make them your great employment; for he that spends his time in sports, and calls it recreation, is like him whose garment is all made of fringes, and his meat nothing but sauces; they are healthless, chargeable, and useless.[20]

Laborare est orare.

Remember,

It is a pleasure to stand upon the shore, and to see ships tost upon the sea; a pleasure to stand in the window of a castle, and to see

If a man love me, he will keep my words.

a battle, and the adventures thereof below; but no pleasure is comparable to the standing upon the vantage-ground of Truth (a hill not to be commanded, and where the air is always clear and serene); and to see the errors and wanderings, and mists and tempests, in the vale below; so always that this prospect be with pity, and not with swelling or pride. Certainly it is heaven upon earth to have a man's mind move in charity, rest in Providence, and turn upon the poles of truth.[65]

REMEMBER,

"Elias was a man of like passions as we are," says St. James, to wean Christians from that false idea which makes us reject the examples of the saints as disproportioned to our own condition. "These were saints," we cry, "and not men like us." We look on them as being crowned in glory; and now that time has cleared up things, it does really appear so. But at the time when the great Athanasius was persecuted, he was a man who bore that name; and St. Teresa, in her day, was like other religious sisters of her order.[112]

One day with thee is as a thousand years, and a thousand years as one day.

REMEMBER,

Time sadly overcometh all things, and is now dominant, and sitteth upon a sphinx, and looketh unto Memphis and old Thebes, while his sister Oblivion reclineth semi-somnous on a pyramid, gloriously triumphing, making puzzles of Titanian erections, and turning old glories into dreams. History sinketh beneath her cloud. The traveller, as he passeth amazedly through those deserts, asketh of her, Who builded them? and she mumbleth something, but what it is he heareth not.[18]

Remember and rejoice, "in the dark hour, that thy life dwells in the midst of a wider and larger life. The earth-clod of the globe has been divinely breathed upon...... The sea of time glitters like the sea of space, with countless beings of light; death and resurrection are the valleys and mountains of the ever-swelling ocean. There exists no dead anatomy; what seems to be such is only another body. Without a universal living existence, there would be nothing but a wide, all-encompassing death. We cling like mosses to the Alps of nature, drawing life from the high clouds, ... and the fly of a day

Let your speech be always with grace, seasoned with salt.

may retrace its infinite series of progenitors, to those first beings of its kind which played over the waters of Paradise before the evening sun."[34]

REMEMBER.

If there is any person to whom you feel dislike, that is the person of whom you ought never to speak."[113]

Forget not the words of Sir Thomas Browne: "There is no man of so discordant and jarring a temper, to which a tunable disposition may not strike a harmony."

> 'T is a kind of good deed to say well;
> And yet words are no deeds.[50]

REMEMBER.

Expression is a sacred thing; it comes free only out of deep and rich experiences; it is forced at the peril of a man's soul; it is wrung out of him only at the price of the spoiling of his nature. Perhaps the rarest gift that God confers upon a man is the power of interesting, quickening, or elevating other men by the utterance of his thoughts, especially upon subjects spiritual and eternal, when they touch no living passion.

He that hath ears to hear let him hear.

It is not to *think* of these things that is unnatural or an effort, but to think of them with the view of one's thoughts passing into words, that they may raise to spring-tides the living waters that lie latent in the cells of other men's souls. It is this, to have to think and *feel with a view to others*, that so often stops thought itself, breaks its living flow, and curdles and taints the emotion, by the reflection of how it is to be used. The desire for the utterance of a man's spirit in any deep direction is intermittent, and, even to the richest nature and most sympathizing heart, can only be occasional.[114]

There is great force hidden in a sweet command.

REMEMBER.

A man that is of judgment and understanding shall sometimes hear ignorant men differ, and know well within himself that those which so differ mean one thing, and yet they themselves would never agree. And if it come so to pass, in that distance of judgment which is between man and man, shall not we think that God above, that knows the heart, doth not discern that frail men, in some of their contra-

Now we see through a glass darkly, but then face to face.

dictions, intend the same thing, and accepteth of both?"[33]

REMEMBER,

St. Gregory reckons sadness — "the sadness of the world, worldly sorrow" — among the seven capital sins; and we read in the Meditations for the English College at Lisbon, "Sadness proceedeth from self-love; and joy, from the love of God."

> There are briers besetting every path,
>   Which call for patient care;
> There is a cross in every lot,
>   And an earnest need for prayer;
> But a lowly heart, that leans on Thee,
>   Is happy anywhere.[113]

The action of the soul is oftener in that which is felt and left unsaid, than in that which is said in any conversation. It broods over every society, and men unconsciously seek for it in each other.[15]

REMEMBER,

De Quincey says, that all our thoughts have not words corresponding to them; many of them, in our imperfectly developed nature, can never express themselves in acts, but must

Star differeth from star in glory.

lie, *appreciable by God only*, like the silent melodies in a great musician's heart, never to roll forth from harp or organ.

Remember,

He who agrees with himself agrees with others.'

Remember,

Nothing recalls the close of life to a noble-hearted young man so much as precisely the happiest and fairest hours which he passes. Gottreich, in the midst of the united fragrance and beauty of the flowers of joy, even with the morning star of life above him, could not but think on the time when the same should appear to him as the evening star, warning him of sleep......
"I will, then," he said, "live through the daytime of truth ·attentively, and bear it away with me to the evening dusk, that it may lighten my end."[34]

Remember,

To live nobly, we must be noble; and we become noble by resolutely banishing every unworthy thought and feeling. This is as

Awake to righteousness.

much a part of a good life as sedulously fulfilling the offices of affection. Some persons feel that devoting the whole life to family duties is the only safe thing. They prize so highly the satisfaction of filling their ideal of life, that they are afraid to enlarge it. Those are bold who willingly narrow it.[116]

Remember

Catherine Adorna, who was in the habit of speaking not only of purity of the heart, but, what is of hardly less importance, of purity of conscience. Sanctification gives to the conscience intensity and multiplicity of existence; so that, like the flaming sword of the cherubim, it turns every way, and guards the tree of life.[117]

Let us keep in mind the Chinese proverb: "Virtue does not give talents, but it supplies their place. Talents neither give virtue nor supply the place of it."

Remember Leigh Hunt's prayer: "May exalting and humanizing thoughts forever accompany me, making me confident without pride, and modest without servility."

Remember,

Man can only learn to rise, from the consideration of that which he cannot surmount.[34]

Thou knowest not what is the way of the spirit.

REMEMBER,

If one listens to the faintest, but constant, suggestions of his genius, which are certainly true, he sees not to what extremes, or even insanity, it may lead him ; and yet that way, as he grows more resolute and faithful, his road lies. . . . . . No man ever followed his genius till it misled him. Though the result were bodily weakness, yet perhaps no one can say that the consequences were to be regretted, for these were a life in conformity with higher principles. If the day and the night are such that you greet them with joy, and life emits a fragrance like flowers and sweet-scented herbs, — is more elastic, more starry, more immortal, — that is your success. All nature is your congratulation, and you have cause momentarily to bless yourself. The greatest gains and values are furthest from being apprehended. We easily come to doubt if they exist. We soon forget them. They are the highest reality. Perhaps the facts most astounding and most real are never communicated by man to man. The true harvest of my daily life is somewhat as in-tangible and indescribable as the tints of morning or evening. It is a little star-dust

Learn of me, for I am meek and lowly.

caught, a segment of a rainbow which I have clutched.[108]

> "For we are hasty builders, incomplete;
> Our Master follows after, far more slow
> And far more sure than we; for frost and heat,
> And winds that breathe, and waters in their flow,
> Work with Him silently."

REMEMBER.

Most natures are insolvent; cannot satisfy their own wants, have an ambition out of all proportion to their practical force, and so do lean and beg day and night continually.[15]

Let us not forget these words of De Sales: "We must never undervalue any person. The workman loves not that his work should be despised in his presence. Now God is present everywhere, and every person is his work."

REMEMBER.

To observe the calmness of great men, noting by the way that real greatness belongs to no station and no set of circumstances. This calmness is the cause of their beautiful behavior. Vanity, injustice, intemperance, are all smallnesses arising from a blindness to proportion in the vain, the unjust, the intemperate. Whereas no one thing, unless it be

Take no thought for the morrow.

the love of God, has such a continuous hold on a great mind as to seem all in all to it.[49]

> Spirit of childhood! loved of God,
> By Jesus' spirit now bestowed,
> How often have I longed for thee;
> O Jesus, form thyself in me!
>
> And help me to become a child
> While yet on earth, meek, undefiled,
> That I may find God always near,
> And Paradise around me here.[118]

REMEMBER.

What is To-morrow until it comes? This moment the evening air thrills with a purple of which no painter as yet has caught the tint, no poet the meaning; no silent face passes in the street on which a human voice might not have charm to call out love and power; the Helper yet waits near. Here is work, life.

Child-souls, you tell me, may find it enough to hold no past and no future, to accept the work of each moment, and think it no wrong to drink every drop of its beauty and joy; we who are wiser laugh at them. It may be; yet I say unto you, their angels only do always behold the face of our Father in the New Year.[119]

Why sleep ye? Arise and pray.

His name was *Care;* a blacksmith by his trade,
That neither day nor night from working spared;
But to small purpose yron wedges made:
Those be unquiet thoughts that careful minds invade.[23]

REMEMBER,

The wise words of one who confessed to himself early one morning, "I am in a very cranky sort of humor; I must take care what I am about to-day." These strange attacks of gloom and restlessness are suddenly and wonderfully alleviated by the interposition of any subject of pleasurable excitement; and for a long period of my life I opposed them after the fashion in which unwise parents quiet a fractious child, by giving it a cake or a new toy; that is to say, I went forth and bought something pretty or pleasant, or wrote a letter, or made a call upon somebody or other; in short, I made an effort to produce a feeling of agreeable excitement in the place of the ennui that disturbed and dissatisfied me. It was really a great many years before I discovered that it was no accidental or trifling disturbance of the moral system which these attacks of restlessness indicated, but that they were the necessary and natural accompaniments of a lapsed spiritual condition.

Be thou faithful unto death.

Well, then, as soon as I had breakfasted, I informed myself that there would be no going to town to-day to buy either books or music, for neither was wanted.

Many persons may say, "Well, suppose you had dissipated your uncomfortable feelings by indulging yourself with the purchase of any little matter you had a fancy for, where would be the harm?" To which I reply, that it is not the mode in which this restlessness of nature acts that is of so much importance as the thing itself. The disease itself is the dreadful thing, and that which is to be fought against.[120]

R*emember*.

Two worlds are ours, one creative of the other. There is the inner realm of thought, emotion, and imagination, and there is the outward realm of practice, where thought, emotion, and imagination take their investiture of flesh and matter, and pass into nature and history. In one we have them in their warmth and fusion, in the other we have them crystallized into fact. All radical changes in character begin in the inner realm of thought and emotion. There we are moved upon by

I will give thee a crown of life.

the powers that are above us; by the Eternal Spirit that lies on our soul like a haunting presence, giving us visions of celestial purity, bitter compunctions, sighs for a better state, and images that float down out of heaven through our fancies. But none of these are yet ours. They sometimes come without any agency of our own. Thus far they have wrought no change in character, for they have not yet passed under the action of a human will. Left to themselves, they are as indeterminate as celestial ethers. They are appropriated by a distinct agency on our part, which consists in giving them a place by our own right arm among fixed and solid realities. The thoughts and emotions wrought in us by the Spirit of God are as yet foreign to us. They are heavenly treasures let down within our grasp. We grasp them by fixing them in the voluntary life, and then they are forever ours.[121]

> The fairest action of our human life
>   Is scorning to revenge an injury;
> For who forgives without a further strife,
>   His adversary's heart to him doth tie.
> And 't is a firmer conquest truly said,
> To win the heart, than overthrow the head.[122]

Be not a forgetful hearer.

Remember,

There's always morning somewhere in the world.[6]

Pythagoras taught that we should avoid and amputate by every possible artifice, by fire and sword, and all various contrivances, from the body, disease; from the soul, ignorance; from the belly, luxury; from a city, sedition; and at the same time, from all things, in moderation. Such, therefore, was the common form of his life at that time, both in words and actions.

Sadi says: "Abu-Horairah was making a daily visit to the prophet Mustafa-Mohammed, on whom be God's blessing and peace. He said, 'O Abu-Horairah, let me alone every other day, that so affection may increase; that is, come not every day, that we may get more loving.'"

Remember,

Wan Tsze always considered a thing three times before he acted. Confucius, hearing of it, said, "Twice may do." (He means Wan Tsze was in danger of wasting time in doubt, or losing spirit in letter.)[123]

Be a doer of the work.

Remember,

Sternness and levity were the two constitutional evils which most severely exercised Mr. Cecil. But so far had grace triumphed over these enemies, that the very opposite features were the most prominent in his character, and no one could approach him without feeling himself with a most *tender* and *serious* mind.[113]

Remember,

The spoken word, the written poem, is said to be an epitome of the man; how much more the done work. Whatsoever of morality and intelligence, what of patience, perseverance, faithfulness, of method, insight, ingenuity, energy, in a word, whatsoever of strength the man had in him will be written in the work he does.

Great honor to him whose Epic is a melodious hexameter Iliad. But still greater honor if his Epic be a mighty empire slowly built together, a mighty series of heroic deeds, — a mighty conquest over chaos. There is no mistaking this latter Epic. Deeds are greater than words. Deeds have such a life, mute but undeniable, and grow as living trees and

The glory of the terrestrial.

fruit-trees do: they people the vacuity of Time, and make it green and worthy.[36]

REMEMBER,

Persons first, we are wont to consider, and books next, in the order of influence. But both disappoint and deceive more or less, — Nature taking the larger share in our culture. Books aid us as we have the skill to use them to advantage; persons best by indirect means, as if they served us not. Nature converts us to ourselves, and against our knowledge or consent.

Nature is the armory of genius. Cities serve it slightly, books and colleges chiefly as they celebrate Nature. She is the first school of eloquence; her images bait the senses to pluck free and fair the befitting rhetoric. A good writer is a pensioner of sun and stars, of fields, woodlands, water, skies, the spectacle of things; agencies these more than libraries or universities, competing successfully for the prizes of inspiration. Whoever would strike effective strokes for truth and ideas, for the times, must be afoot often and early to import the stuff of things into his thoughts, — the sprightliness and point that tell tenderly

Jesus went through the corn-fields on the Sabbath day.

and deeply upon the soul of mankind. "A-field all summer, and the winter spent in studies indoors," is the good Anglo-Saxon rule, and as good for the Anglo-American of to-day. We must take the seasons into us, drinking off their cup daily, if we will live in earnest, and take life with the zest that life is, and the health it gives. For never is the mind weaned from nature or ideas; pasturing at these meadows, she plucks their fruits unrestrained, loving to be abroad musing and amused.[25]

> I care not, fortune, what you me deny,
>   You cannot rob me of free Nature's grace,
> You cannot shut the windows of the sky,
>   Through which Aurora shows her brightening face,
> You cannot bar my constant feet to trace
>   The woods and lawns by living stream at eve.
> Let health my nerves and finer fibres brace,
>   And I their toys to the great children leave;
>   Of fancy, reason, virtue, naught can me bereave.[124]

REMEMBER.

In this world there is one godlike thing, the essence of all that ever was or ever will be of godlike in this world; the veneration done to human worth by the hearts of men.[36]

REMEMBER.

The graces of behavior spring from a sense

We have borne the image of the earthy.

of beauty planted in all minds, even the meanest, and its prevalence is the symptom of a genial culture, distinguishing man or child from the brute he were otherwise. There is a fine religion, or the seed and scion of sanctity, seen in that blushing diffidence by which the loveliest souls are characterized and shown, unconsciously to themselves, by implication. A bashful child is still in Paradise, while the flush of innocency mantles the cheeks, and the maid is apparent there.

It is useless, I should say impious, to clothe for show merely; as useless to teach manners as to give innocence; we must guard and keep the last, that the graces of good behavior may maintain the gloss of their own, and be fine manners indeed, — an emanation of the soul, and the gesture of the mind; self-respect and sensibility being their groundwork and showing. While the child is pure, the person innocent, there is the fine behavior of necessity and the natural piety that graces its owner as counterfeit piety cannot. Good hearts are always graceful, and take captive against any blemishes of nature.[25]

> Stately is service accepted, but lovelier service rendered,
> Interchange of service the law and condition of beauty;
> Any way beautiful only to be the thing one is meant for.

Have not the faith of Christ with respect to persons.

REMEMBER,

Wisdom will never let us stand with any man or men on an unfriendly footing. We refuse sympathy and intimacy with people, as if we waited for some better sympathy and intimacy to come. But whence and when? To-morrow will be like to-day. Life wastes itself while we are preparing to live. . . . . . Let us suck the sweetness of those affections and consuetudes that grow near us. Undoubtedly we can easily pick faults in our company, can easily whisper names prouder, and that tickle the fancy more. Every man's imagination hath its friend; and pleasant would life be with such companions. But if you cannot have them on good mutual terms, you cannot have them. If not the Deity, but our ambition, hews and shapes the new relations, their virtue escapes, as strawberries lose their flavor in garden-beds.[15]

Your little child is your only true democrat.[17]

REMEMBER.

Love, like the opening of the heavens to the saints, shows for a moment, even to the dullest man, the possibilities of the human race. He has faith, hope, and charity for an-

If ye have respect to persons, ye commit sin.

other being, perhaps but a creation of his imagination; still it is a great advance for a man to be profoundly loving even in his imaginations."[49]

Remember.

Be not anxious about those enjoyments which result from the society of accomplished and intellectual persons. There is a subtle snare in everything that appeals to the mind on the side of its tendency to self-glorification and its capacity for estimating talent; and we never think *less* of ourselves for being in association with gifted persons. Seek delight in that which meekens rather than exalts your mind. Keep a watchful eye over yourself on the side of your disposition to self-exaltation.[120]

So Love doth loathe disdainfull nicitee.[28]

Remember.

Form no connections too close with any who live only in the atmosphere of admiration and praise. The love or the friendship of such people rarely contracts itself into the narrow circle of individuals. You, if you are brilliant like themselves, they will hate; you, if you are dull, they will despise. Gaze, therefore, on

Watch, therefore.

the splendor of such idols as a passing stranger. Look for a moment as one sharing in the idolatry; but pass on before the splendor has been sullied by human frailty, or before your own generous homage has been confounded with offerings of weeds.[69]

> Nightly we pitch our moving tents
> A day's march nearer home.[90]

REMEMBER.

Heaven is first a temper, and then a place.[123]

The ripeness, or unripeness, of the occasion must ever be well weighed; and, generally, it is good to commit the beginnings of all great actions to Argus with his hundred eyes; and the ends to Briareus with his hundred hands; first to watch, and then to speed. For the helmet of Pluto, which maketh the politic man go invisible, is secrecy in the council and celerity in the execution. For when things are once come to the execution, there is no secrecy comparable to celerity; like the motion of a bullet in the air, which flieth so swift as it outruns the eye.[65]

REMEMBER

Nothing but effort for virtues which are *not*, can keep alive virtues which *are*.[116]

ANGEL VOICES.

Give to him that asketh.

>There is not on the earth a soul so base
>　　　But may obtain a place
>　　　In covenanted grace;
>So that forthwith his prayer of faith obtains
>　　　Release of his guilt-stains.
>And first-fruits of the second birth, which rise
>From gift to gift, and reach at length the eternal prize,
>All may save self;—but minds that heavenward tower
>　　　Aim at a wider power,
>　　　Gifts on the earth to shower.
>And this is not at once;—by fastings gained,
>　　　And trials well sustained,
>By pureness, righteous deeds, and toils of love,
>Abidance in the truth and zeal for God above.[145]

REMEMBER,

A lively perception of the transitoriness of earth is an ingredient in all virtuous determination. It is not sour in its effect, it is not at all cloistral, it is not melancholy, it is not disheartening, but quite otherwise.

There are few misfortunes, whether of mind, body, or estate, so dangerous as that disease of the spiritual eye by which it fails in perception of the world evanescence.

"To smell the fresh turf is wholesome for the body; no less are thoughts of immortality a cordial for the soul." To the healthy soul they are cordial; but for the salvation of the luxurious they are an indispensable astringent.[86]

This night thy soul shall be required of thee.

"The tree
Sucks kindlier nurture from a soul enriched
By its own fallen leaves: and man is made,
In heart and spirit, from deciduous hopes
And things that seem to perish."

So live, that, when thy summons comes to join
The innumerable caravan that moves
To that mysterious realm, where each shall take
His chamber in the silent halls of death,
Thou go not, like the quarry-slave at night,
Scourged to his dungeon; but, sustained and soothed
By an unfaltering trust, approach thy grave
Like one who wraps the drapery of his couch
About him, and lies down to pleasant dreams.[85]

PART II.

OF DEATH.

We have the sentence of death in ourselves, that we should not trust in ourselves, but in God who raiseth the dead. — 2 Cor. i. 9.

> Yet it pleased the Lord to bruise him;
> He hath put him to grief. — Isaiah liii.

Have pity upon me, have pity upon me, O ye my friends! for the hand of God hath touched me. — Job.

That which thou sowest is not quickened except it die. — 1 Cor. xv. 36.

Thus saith the Lord, Set thine house in order; for thou shalt die, and not live. — Isaiah xxxviii.

For we must needs die, and are as water spilt on the ground, which cannot be gathered up again; neither doth God respect any person: yet doth he devise means that his banished be not expelled from him. — 2 Sam. xiv. 14.

Put thou my tears into thy bottle: are they not in thy book? — Psalm lvi. 8.

If ye loved me, ye would rejoice, because I go to my Father. — Jesus Christ.

Death gives us sleep, eternal youth, and immortality.[34]

> Death is another life. We bow our heads
> At going out, we think, and enter straight
> Another golden chamber of the King's,
> Larger than this we leave, and lovelier.

Our little systems have their day;
    They have their day and cease to be:
    They are but broken lights of thee,
And thou, O Lord, art more than they.

We have but faith: we cannot know;
    For knowledge is of things we see;
    And yet we trust it comes from thee,
A beam in darkness: let it grow.

Let knowledge grow from more to more,
    But more of reverence in us dwell;
    That mind and soul, according well,
May make one music as before,

But vaster. . . . . .

Forgive my grief for one removed,
    Thy creature, whom I found so fair.
    I trust he lives in thee, and there
I find him worthier to be loved.[4]

Yea, saith the Spirit, that they may rest from their labors.

ANGEL VOICES.

REMEMBER,

The strange perversity of human nature, that we are wont to offer nothing but images of terror, no stars of cheering light, to those who lie imprisoned in the darkness of a sickbed, when the glitter of the dew of life is waxing gray and dim before them. It is indeed hard that lamentations and emotions are frequently vented upon the dying, which would be withheld from the living in all their vigor. ..... There stands no lofty spirit, elevated above the circumstance of sorrow, to conduct the prostrate soul of the sufferer, thirsty for the refreshment of joy, back to the old springtide waters of pious recollection; and so to mingle these with the last ecstasies of life, as to give the dying man a foreboding of his transition to another state. On the contrary, the death-bed is narrowed into a coffin without a lid...... Our exit from life would,

Their works do follow them.

therefore, be greatly more painful than our entrance into it, were it not that our good mother Nature had previously mitigated its sufferings . . . . . (as we learn from those who have recovered from apparent death, and from the demeanor of many dying persons,) the brain is, as it were, inundated and watered by faint eddies of bliss, comparable to nothing upon earth better than to the ineffable sensations felt by a patient under magnetic treatment.[34]

REMEMBER,

There is a voice from the tomb sweeter than song; there is a remembrance of the dead to which we turn even from the charms of the living. These we would not exchange for the song of pleasure or the bursts of revelry.[130]

> With what a marvellous vigor can the soul
> Put forth its hidden strength, looking at Death
> As at an Angel from the courts of God!
> And with what beauty, at the closing hour,
> Will childhood's sweet affections blossom out.[131]

> All heads must come
> To the cold tomb;
> Only the actions of the just
> Smell sweet and blossom in the dust.[129]

Let us wait for salvation.

REMEMBER,
The work of righteousness shall be peace; and the effect of righteousness quietness and assurance forever.

> A life well spent is like a flower
> That had bright sunshine its brief hour;
> It flourished in pure willingness,
> Discovered strongest earnestness,
> Was fragrant for each lightest wind,
> Was of its own particular kind,
> Nor knew a tone of discord sharp;
> Breathed alway like a silver harp,
> And went to immortality,
> A very proper thing to die. [132]

> Our noisy years seem moments in the being
> Of the eternal silence; truths that wake,
> To perish never:
> Which neither listlessness nor mad endeavor,
> Nor man nor boy,
> Nor all that is at enmity with joy,
> Can utterly abolish or destroy. [35]

With what shifts and pains we come into the world we remember not, but 't is commonly found no easy matter to get out of it. Many have studied to exasperate the ways of death, but fewer hours have been spent to soften that necessity. That the smoothest way into the grave is made by bleeding, as common opinion presumeth, beside the sick

Of the day and the hour knoweth no man.

and fainting languors which accompany that effusion, the experiment in Lucan and Seneca will make us doubt.

But to learn to die is better than to study the ways of dying. Death will find some ways to untie or cut the most Gordian knots of life, and make men's miseries as mortal as themselves; whereas evil spirits, as undying substances, are inseparable from their calamities; and, therefore, they everlastingly struggle under their angustias, and, bound up with immortality, can never get out of themselves.[18]

REMEMBER,

The unskilful, unexperienced Christian shrieks out whenever his vessel shakes, thinking it always a danger that the watery pavement is not stable and resident like a rock; and yet all his danger is in himself, none at all from without; for he is indeed moving upon the waters, but fastened to a rock; faith is his foundation, and hope is his anchor, and death is his harbor, and Christ is his pilot, and heaven is his country; and all the evils of poverty, or affronts of tribunals and evil judges, of fears and sadder apprehensions, are but like the loud wind blowing from the right

Why seek ye the living among the dead?

point, they make a noise and drive faster to the harbor; and if we do not leave the ship, and leap into the sea; quit the interest of religion, and run to the securities of the world; cut our cables and dissolve our hopes; grow impatient, and hug a wave, and die in its embraces; we are as safe at sea, safer in the storm which God sends us, than in a calm when we are befriended with the world."

I.

Life and thought have gone away
  Side by side,
Leaving door and windows wide:
Careless tenants they!

II.

All within is dark as night:
In the windows is no light;
And no murmur at the door,
So frequent on its hinge before!

III.

Close the door, the shutters close,
  Or through the windows we shall see
  The nakedness and vacancy
Of the dark deserted house.

IV.

Come away; no more of mirth
  Is here, or merry-making sound.
The house was builded of the earth,
  And shall fall again to ground.

The harvest of the earth is ripe.

v.

Come away; for life and thought
Here no longer dwell;
But in a city glorious —
A great and distant city — have bought
A mansion incorruptible.
Would they could have stayed with us.

REMEMBER.

The harvest must be wherever the Son of Man shall send forth his reapers to gather us in. The little child that, without one questioning thought or fear, resigns itself into their hands, though but an opening bud, is gathered into the harvest of the Lord. The young girl, who, through some mysterious sympathy with them, or some strange monition to the soul, seems to hear the sound of their coming from afar, and, without apprehension or surprise, composes herself for the solemn change, and in perfect trust leaves all she loved on earth, goes already ripe for the harvest.[133]

Whate'er thou lovest, man, that too become thou must;
God, if thou lovest God; Dust, if thou lovest dust.[105]

"I saw in seed-time," said Thomas Fuller, "a husbandman at plough on a very raining day; asking him the reason why he would not rather leave off than labor in such foul

The earth was reaped.

weather, his answer was returned to me in their country rhyme:

> 'Sow beans in the mud,
> And they 'll come up like a wood.'

This could not but remind me of David's expression, 'They that sow in tears shall reap in joy. He that goeth forth and weepeth, bearing precious seed, shall doubtless come again with rejoicing, bringing his sheaves with him.'

'"These last five years have been a wet and woful seed-time to me, and many of my afflicted brethren. Little hope have we, as yet, to come again to our own homes, and in a literal sense now to bring our sheaves, which we see others daily carry away on their shoulders. But if we shall not share in the former or latter harvest here on earth, the third and last in heaven we hope undoubtedly to receive."

> Take them, O Death! and bear away
> Whatever thou canst call thine own;
> Thine image, stamped upon this clay,
> Doth give thee that, but that alone:
>
> Take them, O Grave! and let them lie
> Folded, upon thy narrow shelves,

Thou hast delivered mine eyes from tears.

As garments by the soul laid by,
And precious only to ourselves.

Take them, O great Eternity!
Our little life is but a gust
That bends the branches of thy tree,
And trails its blossoms in the dust![72]

REMEMBER
Those last hours of the German pastor, when his son "would fain have infused the fire of conquest reflected in his own bosom, which like a red evening cloud was announcing a fair dawn to Europe, into that old and once strong heart, but he heard neither word nor question of it...... A dying man knows no present, — nothing but the future and the past.

"Death is beautiful," murmured the old man, "and the parting in Christ." Then he added, more and more emphatically, "O thou blessed God!" until all the other luminaries of life were extinguished, and in his soul there stood nothing but the one sun — God!

At length he raised himself, and, stretching out his arm forcibly, exclaimed: "There are three fair rainbows over the evening sun; I must go after the sun, and pass through with him!" He then fell back, and all was over.[34]

Hearken unto the word of the Lord.

> Hearken to yon fine warbler,
> Singing aloft in the tree;
> Hearest thou, O traveller!
> What he singeth to me?
>
> Not unless God made sharp thine ear
> With sorrows such as mine,
> Out of that delicate lay couldst thou
> Its heavy tale divine. [15]

REMEMBER,

Those — so few! — who walk the earth with ever-present consciousness — all mornings, middays, star-times — that the unknown, which men call heaven, is "close behind this visible scene of things." [174]

> He that has light within his own clear breast
> May sit i' the centre, and enjoy bright day;
> But he that hides a dark soul and foul thoughts
> Benighted walks under the midday sun;
> Himself is his own dungeon. [17]

REMEMBER,

"The sorrow which God appoints is purifying and ennobling, and contains within it a serious joy."

REMEMBER,

> "There is no death to those who know of Life,
> No Time to those who see Eternity."

Jesus wept.

Remember

Moderate lamentation is the right of the dead; excessive grief, the enemy to the living."

Remember.

In the last hour, that pure being with whom thy life was beautiful and great, — with whom thou hast wept tears of joy, with whom thou hast prayed to God, and in whom God appeared unto thee, in whom thou didst find the first and last heart of love, — and then close thine eyes in peace!

. . . . .

"Ay, this day shall we see one another again!" continued the old man; but he spoke of his wife, who was long since dead.

But be one sorrow alone forgiven thee, or made good to thee, — the sorrow for thy dead ones; for this sweet sorrow for the lost is itself but another form of consolation. When the heart is full of longing for them, it is but another mode of continuing to love them; and we shed tears as well when we think of their departure, as when we picture to ourselves our joyful reunion, — and the tears, methinks, differ not."

Thou shalt sleep with thy fathers.

IN DEATH.

I saw an aged man upon his bier,
    His hair was thin and white, and on his brow
A record of the cares of many a year, —
    Cares that were ended and forgotten now.
And there was sadness round, and faces bowed,
And women's tears fell fast, and children wailed aloud!

Then rose another hoary man, and said,
    In faltering accents, to that weeping train,
Why mourn ye that our aged friend is dead?
    Ye are not sad to see the gathered grain,
Nor when their mellow fruit the orchards cast,
Nor when the yellow woods shake down the ripened mast.

Ye sigh not when the sun, his course fulfilled,
    His glorious course, rejoicing earth and sky,
In the soft evening, when the winds are stilled,
    Sinks where his islands of refreshment lie,
And leaves the smile of his departure, spread
O'er the warm-colored heaven and ruddy mountain head.

Why weep ye, then, for him, who, having run
    The bound of man's appointed years, at last,
Life's blessings all enjoyed, life's labors done,
    Serenely to his final rest has passed,
While the soft memory of his virtues yet
Lingers, like twilight hues when the bright sun is set?

His youth was innocent; his riper age
    Marked with some acts of goodness, every day;
And watched by eyes that loved him, calm and sage,
    Faded his late declining years away.
Cheerful he gave his being up, and went
To share the holy rest that waits a life well spent.

I will lay me down in peace and sleep.

That life was happy; every day he gave
    Thanks for the fair existence that was his;
For a sick fancy made him not her slave,
    To mock him with her phantom miseries.
No chronic tortures racked his aged limb,
For luxury and sloth had nourished none for him.

And I am glad that he has lived thus long,
    And glad that he has gone to his reward,
Nor deem that kindly Nature did him wrong
    Softly to disengage the vital cord.
When his weak hand grew palsied, and his eye
Dark with the mists of age, it was his time to die.[85]

REMEMBER,

That, though the realm of Death seems an enemy's country to most men, on whose shores they are loathly driven by stress of weather, to the wise man it is the desired port where he moors his bark gladly, as in some quiet haven of the Fortunate Isles; it is the golden west into which his sun sinks, and, sinking, casts back a glory upon the leaden cloud-rack which had darkly besieged his day.[12]

    The death-bed of the just, —
    Angels should paint it, — Angels ever there!
    There on a post of honor and of joy.[61]

REMEMBER,

There is healing in the bitter cup. God takes away, or removes far from us, those we

Lighten my eyes, lest I sleep the sleep of death.

love, as hostages of our faith (if I may so express it); and to those who look forward to a reunion in another world, where there will be no separation, and no mutability except that which arises from perpetual progressiveness, the evening of life becomes more delightful than the morning, and the sunset offers brighter and lovelier visions than those which we build up in the morning clouds, and which appear before the strength of the day. Faith is that precious alchemy which transmutes grief into joy; or rather, it is the pure and heavenly Euphrasy, which clears away the film from our mortal sight, and makes affliction appear what it really is, a dispensation of mercy.[134]

REMEMBER,

From our mere eyes Death takes only the visible form of the objects of our love, for this is only borrowed; from our souls it cannot take the love itself to which that is subservient, for it is given us forever. The very grief that wastes us testifies that, in his true worth, the companion we lament as lost is with us still; for is it not the idea of him that weeps in us,— his image that supplies the tears? His best offices he will continue to us yet, if

The maid is not dead, but sleepeth.

we are true to him; with serenest look, as through the windows of the soul, rebuking our disquiet, bracing our faith, quickening our conscience, and cooling the fever-heats of life. Doubtless the thought of him is transmuted from gladness into sorrow. But will any true heart say, that an affection is an evil because it is sad, and wish to shake it off the moment it brings pain? Call it what you will, *that* is not love which itself is anxious to grow cold; the emotions of a faithful soul never entertain a suicidal purpose, and plan their own extinction; rather do they reproach their own insensibility, and passionately pray for a greater vitality. Whether, then, in anxiety or in peace, in joy or in regrets, let the spirit of affection stay; and if the spirit stay, the objects, though vanished, leave their best presence with us still. Thus the sainted dead shall finish for us the blessed work which they began. They tarried with us, and nurtured a human love; they depart from us, and kindle a divine.[80]

Death is the crown of life.
Were death denied, poor man would live in vain;
Were death denied, to live would not be life;
Were death denied, even fools would wish to die.
Death wounds to cure; we fall, we rise, we reign,

I sleep, but my heart waketh.

Spring from our fetters, fasten in the skies.
This King of Terrors is the Prince of Peace.
When shall I die to vanity, pain, death?
When shall I die? When shall I live forever?[61]

Remember.

Death is a commingling of eternity with time; in the death of a good man, eternity is seen looking through time.[8]

THE DEAD.

"Still the same, no charm forgot,—
Nothing lost that Time had given."

Forget not the Dead, who have loved, who have left us,
  Who bend o'er us now from their bright homes above;
But believe — never doubt — that the God who bereft us
  Permits them to mingle with friends they still love.

Repeat their fond words, all their noble deeds cherish,
  Speak pleasantly of them who left us in tears; —
Other joys may be lost, but their names should not perish
  While time bears our feet through the valley of years.

Dear friends of our youth! can we cease to remember
  The last look of life, and the low-whispered prayer?
O, cold be our hearts as the ice of December,
  When Love's tablets record no remembrances there!

Then forget not the Dead, who are evermore nigh us,
  Still floating sometimes to our dream-haunted bed; —
In the loneliest hour, in the crowd, they are by us:
  Forget not the dead, — O, forget not the dead![135]

He saith, Our friend Lazarus sleepeth.

Remember.

The word friend is of a large signification; and means all relations and societies, and whatsoever is not enemy. But by friendships, I suppose you mean the greatest love, and the greatest usefulness, and the most open communication, and the noblest sufferings, and the most exemplar faithfulness, and the severest truth, and the heartiest counsel, and the greatest union of minds of which brave men and women are capable.[20]

Remember.

The last and most sacred duty of friendship is after we have stood upon the planks round his grave. When my friend is dead, I will not turn into his grave and be stifled with his earth; but I will mourn for him, and perform his will, and take care of his relatives, and do for him as if he were alive; and thus it is that friendships never die.[136]

> Good night! — now cometh gentle sleep,
>   And tears that fall like gentle rain;
> Good night! O, holy, blest, and deep
>   The rest that follows pain!
> How should we reach God's upper light,
> If life's long day had no "good night"?[17]

ANGEL VOICES.

God hath given to us eternal life.

Leaves and clustered fruits, and flowers eterne,
Eternal to the world, but not to me.[83]

REMEMBER.

The iniquity of oblivion blindly scattereth her poppy, and deals with the memory of men without distinction to merit of perpetuity. Who can but pity the founder of the pyramids? Erostratus lives that burnt the Temple of Diana; he is almost lost that built it. Time hath spared the epitaph of Adrian's horse, confounded that of himself. In vain we compute our felicities by the advantage of our good names, since bad have equal decorations; and Thersites is like to live as long as Agamemnon. Who knows whether the best of men be known; or whether there be not more remarkable persons forgot than any that stand remembered in the known account of time? Without the favor of the everlasting register, the first man had been as unknown as the last, and Methuselah's long life had been his only chronicle.[18]

O eloquent, just, and mighty Death! whom none could advise, thou hast persuaded; what none hath dared, thou hast done; and whom all the world hath flattered, thou only hast

Death is swallowed up in victory.

cast out of the world and despised; thou hast drawn together all the far-stretched greatness, all the pride, cruelty, and ambition of man, and covered it all over with these two narrow words, — *Hic jacet!* [138]

Remember

This fair picture of true piety, drawn by Jeremy Taylor from the life and death of Frances, Countess of Carbery.

"Her religion took root downward in humility, and brought forth fruit upward in the substantial graces of a Christian; in charity and justice; in chastity and modesty; in fair friendships and sweetness of society. She had not very much of the forms and outsides of godliness, but she was hugely careful for the power of it, for the moral, essential, and useful parts, such which would make her to be, not seem to be, religious. . . . . . In all her religion, and in all her actions of relation toward God, she had a strange evenness and untroubled passage, sliding toward her ocean of God and of infinity with a certain and silent motion. . . . . . Though she had the greatest judgment and the greatest experience of things and persons that I ever yet knew in a person of her youth and sex and circumstances; yet, as if

Whither I go thou knowest not now, but thou shalt know hereafter.

she knew nothing of it, she had the meanest opinion of herself, and, like a fair taper, when she shined to all the room, yet round about her own station she had cast a shadow and a cloud, and she shined to everybody but herself.

"..... But so it was that the thought of death dwelt long with her, and grew, from the first steps of fancy and fear, to a consent; from thence, to a strange credulity and expectation of it; and, without the violence of sickness, she died as if she had done it voluntarily and by design, and for fear her expectation should have been deceived, or that she should seem to have had an unreasonable fear or apprehension, or rather (as one said of Cato) she died as if she were glad of the opportunity."

REMEMBER.

Happy are they which live not in that disadvantage of time, when men could say little for futurity but from reason; whereby the noblest minds fell often upon doubtful deaths and melancholy dissolutions. With those hopes Socrates warmed his doubtful spirits against that cold potion; and Cato, before he durst give the fatal stroke, spent part of the night in reading the immortality of Plato, thereby

I am the life.

confirming his wavering hand unto the animosity of that attempt.[18]

Death, thou wast once an uncouth, hideous thing;
. . . .
But since our Saviour's death
Has put some blood into thy face,
Thou hast grown sure a thing to be desired
And full of grace.[70]

REMEMBER.

There is a countrie
Afar beyond the stars
Where stands a wingèd sentrie
All skilfull in the wars.
There, above noise and danger,
Sweet Peace sits crowned with smiles,
And One born in a manger
Commands the beauteous files.
He is thy gracious friend,
And (O my soul, awake!)
Did in pure love descend,
To die here for thy sake.
If thou canst get but thither,
There growes the flowre of peace,
The Rose that cannot wither,
Thy fortresse, and thy ease.[64]

REMEMBER.

Grief is only the memory of widowed affection. The more intense the delight in the presence of the object, the more poignant must be the impression of the absence. . . . . .

Blessed are they that mourn.

These associations with the past do not excite sorrow, but to an affectionate mind are sorrow. The morality, then, which rebukes sorrow, rebukes love. There are doubtless cases not infrequent, in which the mind is unduly overpowered by affliction, in which the tranquillity of the reason is wholly overset, and the energy of the will utterly prostrated. Here, beyond controversy, is a state of mind morally wrong; for God never absolves us from our duties, however he may sadden them. But to rebuke the feelings of grief in such a case is to cast the censure in the wrong place: it is not that the sorrow is excessive, but that other emotions are defective in their strength.

The wise interpreter of his own nature will let his mourning affections alone. To interfere with them would be to wrestle with his own strength. But he will draw forth into prominent light sentiments now sleeping idly in the shaded recesses of his mind. He will summon up the sense of responsibility, to rouse him with the spectacle of his relations to God, his father, and his brother, man; to recount to him the deeds of duty and the toils of thought which are yet to be achieved ere life is done; to show him the circle of high

They shall be comforted.

faculties which the Creator has given him to ennoble and refine and keep ready for a world where thought and virtue are immortalized. He will call forth his affections for the living who surround him, and whom yet it is happiness to love and his obligation to bless; and these sympathies will be fruitful work for his hands, and interests refreshing to his heart; here are some of the invitations to the aspirings of benevolence, to bid the drooping soul look up. And the sufferer will evoke the spirit of Christian trust and hope. Invoke the spirit of this trust; and though sorrow may not dry its tears, it rises to a dignity above despair.[80]

REMEMBER,
He whose mission it was to teach the paternity of Providence and the serenity of the immortal hope,—he who himself lived in the divinest peace which they can give, thought it no treason to these truths to weep. To the eye of the Man of Sorrows, sorrow was no sin; nor did he, who was emphatically the Son of God, see in even the passionate utterance of grief any of that spirit of filial distrust towards God, and reluctant acceptance of his will, which have often been charged on it by

A man of sorrows and acquainted with grief.

the hard and cold temper of his followers, who would multiply the penances of natural emotion, and sublime from the Gospel its pure humanities.[82]

Be sure that God
Ne'er dooms to waste the strength he deigns to impart.[14]

REMEMBER,

Heaven and God are best discerned through tears; scarcely, perhaps, are discerned at all without them. The constant association of prayer with the hour of bereavement and the scenes of death suffices to show this. Yet is this effect of external distress only a particular instance of this general truth, that religion springs up in the mind wherever any of the infinite affections and desires press severely against the finite conditions of our existence. Instead of slumbering at noon in Eden, we must keep the midnight watch within Gethsemane. We, too, like our great Leader, must be made perfect through suffering; but the struggle by night will bring the calmness of the morning; the hour of exceeding sorrow will prepare the day of godlike strength; the prayer for deliverance calls down the power of endurance. And while to the reluctant their cross is too heavy to be borne, it grows light to the heart of willing trust.[83]

The Lord gave, and the Lord hath taken away:

"She died young."
"I think not so; her infelicity
Seemed to have years too many." [1,9]

REMEMBER.

When in the other world love meets love, it will not be like Joseph and his brethren, who lay upon one another's necks weeping; it will be loving and rejoicing, not loving and sorrowing. [140]

Endure and dare, true heart, through patience joined
With boldness come we at a crown enriched
With thousand blessings. [141]

REMEMBER

The hour of death, — dark hour to hopeless unbelief! hour to which, in that creed of despair, no hour shall succeed! being's last hours! to whose appalling darkness, even the shadows of an avenging retribution were brightness and relief, — death! what art thou to the Christian's assurance? Great hour of answer to life's prayer, great hour that shall break asunder the bond of life's mystery, — hour of release from life's burden, — hour of reunion with the loved and lost, — what mighty hopes hasten to their fulfilment in thee! What longings, what aspirations, breathed in the still night, beneath the silent stars; what dread emotions of curiosity; what deep meditations

---
Blessed be the name of the Lord.
---

of joy; what hallowing imaginings of never experienced purity and bliss; what possibilities shadowing forth unspeakable realities to the soul, — all verge to their consummation in thee, O death! the Christian's death! what art thou, but the gate of life, the portal of heaven, the threshold of eternity![142]

> They are not lost
> Who leave their parents for the calm of heaven.
> .   .   .   .   .   I know well
> That they who love their friends most tenderly
> Still bear their loss the best. There is in love
> A consecrated power, that seems to wake
> Only at the touch of death from its repose,
> In the profoundest depths of thinking souls,
> Superior to the outward signs of grief,
> Sighing or tears, — when these have past away,
> It rises calm and beautiful, like the moon,
> Saddening the solemn night, yet with that sadness
> Mingling the breath of undisturbed peace.[143]

Remember,

There is nothing greater, for which God made our tongues, next to reciting his praises, than to minister comfort to a weary soul. And what greater measure can we have, than that we should bring joy to our brother, who with his dreamy eyes looks to heaven, and round about, and cannot find so much rest as to lay his eyelids close together, — than that

Rejoice with them that do rejoice, and weep with them that weep.

thy tongue should be tuned with heavenly accents, and make the weary soul to listen for light and ease, and, when he perceives that there is such a thing in the world, and in the order of things, as comfort and joy, to begin to break out from the prison of his sorrows? ..... So have I seen the sun kiss the frozen earth, which was bound up with the images of death, and the colder breath of the north; and then the waters break from their enclosures, and melt with joy, and run in useful channels; and the flies do rise again from their little graves in walls, and dance awhile in the air, to tell that there is joy within. ..... So is the heart of a sorrowful man under the discourses of a wise comforter; he breaks from the despairs of the grave, and the fetters and chains of sorrow; he blesses God, and he blesses thee, and he feels his life returning; for to be miserable is death, but nothing is life but to be comforted; and God is pleased with no music from below so much as in the thanksgiving songs of relieved widows, of supported orphans, of rejoicing and comforted and thankful persons.[20]

REMEMBER.

If the nearness of our last necessity brought

I die daily.

a nearer conformity unto it, there were a happiness in hoary hairs, and no calamity in half senses. But the long habit of living indisposeth us for dying; when avarice makes us the sport of death, when even David grew politically cruel, and Solomon could hardly be said to be the wisest of men. But many are too early old, and before the date of age. Adversity stretcheth our days; misery makes Almena's nights (one night as long as three), and time hath no wings unto it.[18]

> God! whom I as Love have known,
> Thou hast sickness laid on me,
> And these pains are sent of Thee.
>
> . . . . .
>
> In my weakness be Thou strong,
>   Be Thou sweet when I am sad,
>   Let me still in Thee be glad,
> Though my pains be keen and long.
>
> . . . . .
>
> Suffering is the work now sent,
>   Nothing can I do but lie
>   Suffering as the hours go by:
> All my powers to this are bent,
> Suffering is my gain; I bow,
>   To my Heavenly Father's will,
>   And receive it hushed and still;
> Suffering is my worship now.[118]

Remember.

    It is the heaviest stone that melancholy can

Behold, we count them happy who endure.

throw at a man, to tell him he is at the end of his nature: or that there is no further state to come, unto which this seems progressional, and otherwise made in vain. Without this accomplishment, the natural expectation and desire of such a state were but a fallacy in nature.

But the superior ingredient and obscured part of ourselves, whereto all present felicities afford no resting contentment, will be able at last to tell us we are more than our present selves, and evacuate such hopes on the fruition of their own accomplishment.[18]

> High hopes, that burned like stars sublime,
> Go down the heavens of Freedom;
> And true hearts perish in the time
> We bitterliest need them!
> But never sit we down and say
> There's nothing left but sorrow;
> We walk the wilderness to-day,
> The promised land to-morrow.
>
> Build up heroic lives, and all
> Be like a sheathen sabre,
> Ready to flash out at God's call,
> O chivalry of labor!
> Triumph and toil are twins; and aye
> Joy suns the cloud of sorrow; —
> And 't is the martyrdom to-day
> Brings victory to-morrow.[144]

All that a man hath will he give for his life.

REMEMBER,

This is that very life which Christ asks us to lay down for him; this life of which he tells us that he who loveth it shall lose it, and he who loseth it for his sake shall keep it unto life eternal.[56]

>Upward steals the life of man,
>As the sunshine from the wall;
>From the wall into the sky;
>From the roof along the spire.
>Ah! the souls of those that die
>Are but sunbeams lifted higher.[73]

We ought to love life; we ought to desire to live here so long as God ordains it; but let us not so encase ourselves in time that we cannot break the crust and begin to throw out shoots for another life.[145]

Remember the touching words of Southey in recalling the fear expressed by Henry Kirke White, "that early death would rob him of his fame."

Just at that age when the painter would have wished to fix his likeness, and the lover of poetry would delight to contemplate him, in the fair morning of his virtues, the full spring blossom of his hopes, — just at that age *hath death set the seal of eternity* upon

We are as the grass of the field.

him, and the *beautiful hath been made permanent.*

My joy is *Death!*
Death, at whose name I oft have been afeared,
Because I wished this world's eternity.[50]

REMEMBER.

It is as natural to die as to be born; and to a little child, perhaps, the one is as painful as the other. He that dies in an earnest pursuit is like one that is wounded in hot blood, who for the time scarce feels the hurt; and therefore a mind fixed and bent upon somewhat that is good doth avert the dolors of death. But above all, believe it, the sweetest canticle is "Nunc dimittis" when a man hath obtained worthy aims and expectations. Death hath this also,—that it openeth the gate of fame, and extinguisheth envy.[65]

The glories of our birth and state
Are shadows, not substantial things;
There is no armor against fate;
Death lays his icy hands on kings;
Sceptre and crown
Must tumble down,
And in the dust be equal made
With the poor crooked scythe and spade.[120]

REMEMBER.

The iniquity of oblivion blindly scattereth

Rejoice evermore.

her poppy, and deals with the memory of men without distinction to merit of perpetuity. ..... In vain we compute our felicities by the advantage of our good names, since bad have equal duration. ..... Oblivion is not to be hired. The greater part must be content to be as though they had not been, to be found in the register of God, not in the record of men. ..... The night of time far surpasseth the day: and who knows when was the equinox?[16]

Like a common weed
The sea-swell took her hair.[38]

Remember.

Were the happiness of the next world as closely apprehended as the felicities of this, it were a martyrdom to live; and unto such as consider none hereafter, it must be more than death to die, which makes us amazed at those audacities that durst be nothing, and return into their chaos again.

But the contempt of death from corporal animosity promoteth not our felicity. They may sit in the orchestra and noblest seats of heaven who have held up shaking hands in the fire, and humanly contended for glory.[18]

Ye now have sorrow; but I will see you again.

O Light of light celestial!
O charity ineffable!
Come in thy hidden majesty;
Fill us with love, fill us with Thee.[146]

Courage! ye that bear the sublime lot of sorrow! It is not forever that ye suffer. God wills it. It is the ordinance of Infinite Love to procure for us an infinite glory and beatitude.[142]

REMEMBER,

The greatness of our sufferings points to a correspondent greatness in the end to be gained. This end must rise higher and brighter before us, before we can look through the dark cloud of human calamity. . . . . . Troubles, disappointments, afflictions, sorrows, press us on every side, that we may rise upward, upward, ever upward. . . . . . Misery, strictly speaking, and in its full meaning, does not belong to a good mind. Misery shall pass into suffering, and suffering into discipline, and discipline into virtue, and virtue into heaven. So let it pass with you. Bend now patiently and meekly in that lowly "worship of sorrow," till in God's time it become the worship of joy. . . . . . Remember, too, a *man* of sorrows was that Divine Master, and

It is expedient for you that I go away.

acquainted with grief. And what were the instruments, the means, the ministers of that very victory,— that last victory? The rage of men, and the fierceness of torture; arraignment before enemies,— mocking, smiting, scourging; the thorny crown, the bitter cross, the barred tomb. . . . . . When I stand in the presence of that high example, I cannot listen to poor, unmanly, unchristian complainings. I would not have his disciples account too much of their griefs.

REMEMBER,

Astronomers have built telescopes which can show myriads of stars unseen before; but when a man looks through a tear in his own eye, that is a lens which opens, reaches in the unknown, and reveals orbs which no telescope, however skilfully constructed, could do; nay, which brings to view even the throne of God, and pierces that nebulous distance where are those eternal verities in which true life consists.[145]

> Silent rushes the swift Lord
> Through ruined systems still restored,
> Broad-sowing, bleak and void to bless,
> Plants with worlds the wilderness,
> Waters with tears of ancient sorrow
> Apples of Eden ripe to-morrow.[15]

Thou in faithfulness hast afflicted me.

REMEMBER.

Suffering is a part of the Divine idea. All new faculties stand in a double constitution, and are just as really susceptible of pain as of pleasure. We were created so that every nerve was provided with this twofold nature, and both of them are divine. The world is filled full of dangerous things, — things which can bruise and cut and poison, — and no angel stands near them to say, "Come not here." There is not a step we take but death is there. Pain is continually on the larboard or starboard side, and life consists in steering between dangers on the one hand or the other. Where there is so much sorrow, there is only one way. It is to think that suffering is a part of happiness. One who does this takes all trials, and heaps them up, and says, "They are no longer to me what they were before. They are not opaque, they are luminous."[145]

> How fresh, O Lord, how sweet and clear
> Are thy returns ! e'en as the flowers in spring ;
> To which, besides their own demean,
> The late past frosts tributes of pleasure bring.
> Grief melts away
> Like snow in May,
> As if there were no such cold thing.[76]

Blessed is the man who, when the tempest

I will allure her and bring her into the wilderness.

has spent its fury, recognizes his Father's voice in its under-tone, and bares his head and bows his knee, as Elijah did. To such . . . . . it seems as if God had said: "In the still sunshine and ordinary ways of life you cannot meet me, but like Job in the desolation of the tempest you shall see My Form and hear My Voice, and know that your Redeemer liveth."

If ever failure seemed to rest on a noble life, it was when the Son of Man, deserted by his friends, heard the cry which proclaimed that the Pharisees had successfully drawn the net round their Divine Victim. Yet from that very hour of defeat and death there went forth the world's life, — from that very moment of apparent failure there proceeded forth into the ages the spirit of the conquering Cross. Surely if the Cross says anything, it says that apparent defeat is real victory, and that there is a heaven for those who have *nobly* and *truly* failed on earth.'"

Remember the words of Robert Southwell when awaiting martyrdom. We have sung the canticles of the Lord in a strange land, and in this desert we have sucked honey from the rock, and oil from the hard stone; but

Be strong, and He shall comfort thine heart.

"we now sow the seed with tears, that others hereafter may with joy carry in the sheaves to the heavenly granaries."

> O Time! O Death! I clasp you in my arms,
> For I can soothe an infinite cold sorrow,
> And gaze contented on your icy charms,
> And that wild snow-pile, which we call to-morrow;
> Sweep on, O soft and azure-lidded sky,
> Earth's waters to your gentle gaze reply.
>
> I am not earth-born, though I here delay;
> Hope's child, I summon infiniter powers,
> And laugh to see the mild and sunny day
> Smile on the shrunk and thin autumnal hours;
> I laugh, for hope hath happy place with me,
> If my bark sinks, 't is to another sea.[132]

REMEMBER,

Although the fig-tree shall not blossom, neither shall fruit be in the vines; the labor of the olive shall fail, and the fields shall yield no meat; the flock shall be cut off from the fold, and there shall be no herd in the stalls; yet I will rejoice in the Lord, I will joy in the God of my salvation. — *Habakkuk.*

REMEMBER,

God sees sin not in its consequences, but in itself; a thing infinitely evil, even if the consequences were happiness to the guilty instead of misery. So sorrow, according to God, is

Lord, thou knowest all things.

to see sin as God sees it. The grief of Peter was as bitter as that of Judas. He went out and wept bitterly; how bitterly none can tell but they who have learned to look on sin as God does. But in Peter's grief there was an element of hope; and that sprung precisely from this,—that he saw God in it all. Despair of self did not lead to despair of God. ..... I believe the feeling of true penitence would express itself in such words as these: — there *is* a righteousness, though I have not attained it. There is a purity and a love and a beauty, though my life exhibits little of it. In that I can rejoice. Of that I can feel the surpassing loveliness. My doings? They are worthless; I cannot endure to think of them. I am not thinking of them. I have something else to think of. There, There; in that Life I see it. And so the Christian — gazing, not on what he is, but on what he desires to be — dares in penitence to say, That righteousness is mine; dares, even when the recollection of his sin is most vivid and most poignant, to say, with Peter, thinking less of himself than of God, and sorrowing as it were with God, "Lord, thou knowest all things, thou knowest that I love thee."[147]

And Enoch walked with God: and he was not, for God took him.

REMEMBER,

To be content with death may be better than to desire it; a miserable life may make us wish for death, but a virtuous one to rest in it: which is the advantage of those resolved Christians, who, looking on death not only as the sting, but the period and end of sin, the horizon and isthmus between this life and a better, and the death of this world but as a nativity of another, do contentedly submit unto the common necessity, and envy not Enoch or Elias.[18]

We go to the grave of a friend saying, "A man is dead," but the angels throng about him, saying, A man is born.[145]

> Build thee more stately mansions, O my soul,
>   As the swift seasons roll!
>   Leave thy low-vaulted past!
> Let each new temple, nobler than the last,
> Shut thee from heaven with a dome more vast,
>   Till thou at length art free,
> Leaving thine out-grown shell by life's unresting sea.[143]

> God's saints are shining lights: who stays
>   Here long must passe
> O're dark hills, swift streams, and steep ways
>   As smooth as glasse:
>   But these all night,
>   Like candles, shed
>   Their beams, and light
>   Us into bed.[54]

Thy love to me was wonderful.

REMEMBER,

Our sweetest experiences of affection are meant to be suggestions of that realm which is the home of the heart.[145]

REMEMBER,

There are questions which nothing can answer but God's love; which nothing can meet but God's promise; which nothing can calm but a perfect trust in his goodness. Speak to the void darkness of affliction, "the first dark day of nothingness" after trouble has come; speak to life through all its stages and fortunes, from oftentimes suffering infancy to trembling age, ... none of these can answer us. . . . . . There is shadow and mystery upon all the creation till we see God in it; there is trouble and fear till we see God's love in it.[142]

> How my cup o'erlooks her brims!
> So, even so still may I move
> By the line of thy dear love;
> Still may thy sweet mercy spread
> A shady arm above my head,
> About my paths; so shall I find
> The fair centre of my mind,
> Thy temple, and those lovely walls
> Bright ever with a beam that falls
> Fresh from the pure glance of Thine eye,
> Lighting to Eternity.[143]

Into thy hand I commit my spirit.

REMEMBER,

In the hour of death, faith will be our only availing possession. How many persons mistake, as though innocent recollections would be support enough! And how many Pharisees imagine the blessedness of looking back from their death-beds upon years of intense hatred, borne unremittingly against what they call the world, namely, their fellow-men and their pleasures! But faith is not formed out of hatred, not even of Satan; it is a nobler fruit; it springs out of love, — that love of God which is so strong as to believe all things, and, concerning the very worst, to hope all things; it is "Christ in you the hope of glory"; it is the essence of many prayers; it is the state of a pure heart. At death all other possessions fail us. Interest in the surrounding world declines; reflection is enfeebled; and sensation fails. The light of genius is sometimes so resplendent as to make a man walk through life, amid glory and acclamation; but it burns very dimly and low when carried into "the valley of the shadow of death." But faith is like the evening star, shining into our souls the more brightly, the deeper is the night of death in which they sink.[86]

It is I; be not afraid.

> I placed thee in a land of light,
> Where the Gospel round thee shone:
> Where is the heavenly-mindedness
> I find in all mine own?
> And last I "sent thee chastisement,"
> That thou might'st be my son:
> Where is the trusting faith which says,
> "Father! thy will be done"? [105]

In death remember Christ, — how, interpenetrated by his spirit, thy soul was born again, and, blessed token thereof, calamity itself counted all joy, — how through him the forms and the vicissitudes of nature have, in thy sight, grown significant of a holier philosophy than that anciently so called, — how, upon this earth, thou hast been shown the Father, and, amid earth's disorders and darkness, it hath sufficed thee. . . . . . Life, as far as it has been life, hath it not been through Christ? and death, is not that the sure coming of Christ? [86]

> A blissful vision through the night
>   Would all my happy senses sway,
> Of the Good Shepherd on the height,
>   Or climbing up the stony way,
>
> Holding our little lamb asleep,
>   And like the burden of the sea
> Sounded that voice along the deep,
>   Saying, "Arise and follow me." [149]

Though I walk through the valley of the shadow of death,

R*EMEMBER*.

Death meets us everywhere, and is procured by every instrument, and in all chances, and enters in at many doors, by violence and secret influence, by the aspect of a star and the stink of a mist, by the emissions of a cloud and the melting of a vapor, by the fall of a chariot and the stumbling at a stone, by a full meal or an empty stomach, by watching at the wine or by watching at prayers, by the sun or the moon, by a heat or a cold, by sleepless nights or sleeping days, by water frozen into the hardness and sharpness of a dagger, or water thawed into the floods of a river, by a hair or a raisin, by violent motion or sitting still, by severity or dissolution, by God's mercy or God's anger.

The chains that confine us to this condition are strong as destiny and immutable as the eternal laws of God.[20]

> To wandering men how dear the sight
> Of a cold, tranquil autumn night,
>   In its majestic, deep repose.
>   Thus shall their genius be
>   Not buried in high snows,
> Though of as mute tranquillity.
>
> An anxious life they will not pass,
> Nor, as the shadow on the grass,

I will fear no evil.

    Leave no impression there to stay :
        To them all things are thought ;
        The blushing morn's decay,
Our death, our life, by this is taught.

O find in every haze that shines
A brief appearance without lines,
A single word, — no finite joy ;
    For present is a Power
    Which we may not annoy,
Yet love him stronger every hour.

I would not put this sense from me,
If I could some great sovereign be ;
Yet will not task a fellow-man
    To feel the same glad sense ;
    For no one living can
Feel, save his given influence.[132]

REMEMBER the words of Richter :

If ever my heart were so unhappy and withered, that all the feelings which assert the existence of God should be destroyed, I would terrify myself with this my essay, and it would heal me, and give me my feelings back again. ..... One summer evening I lay upon a mountain in the sunshine, and fell asleep. ..... I saw one corpse alone, which had just been buried in the church, lying still upon its pillow, and its breast heaved not, while upon its smiling countenance lay a happy dream ; but on the entrance of one of

Under the cloud and through the sea.

the living shadows he awoke, and smiled no more. He opened his closed eyes with a painful effort, but within there was no eye; and in the sleeping bosom, instead of a heart, there was a wound. . . . . . A lofty, noble form, having the expression of a never-ending sorrow, now sank down from above upon the altar, and all the dead exclaimed, "Christ! is there no God?" And he answered, "There is none!" The whole shadow of each dead one, and not the breast alone, now trembled, and one after another was severed by the trembling. . . . . . Then there arose and came into the temple — a terrible sight for the heart! — the dead children who had awakened in the churchyard, and they cast themselves before the lofty form upon the altar, and said, "Jesus! have we no Father?" And he answered with streaming eyes, "We are all orphans, I and you: we are without a Father." . . . . .

Here Christ looked towards the earth and said: "Alas! I too was once like you: . . . . . too happy dwellers of earth, ye still believe in him! . . . . . When the man of sorrows stretches his sore-wounded back upon the earth to slumber towards a lovelier morning,

The righteous perisheth, and no man layeth it to heart.

full of truth, full of virtue and of joy, behold he wakes in the tempestuous chaos, in the everlasting midnight, and no morning cometh, and no healing hand, and no Infinite Father. Mortal who art near me, if thou still livest, worship him, or thou hast lost him forever!"

And as I fell down and gazed into the gleaming fabric of worlds, I beheld the raised rings of the giant serpent of eternity, which had couched itself round the universe of worlds, and the rings fell, and she enfolded the universe doubly. Then she wound herself in a thousand folds round Nature, and crushed the worlds together, and, grinding them, she squeezed the infinite temple into the churchyard church, — and all became narrow, dark, and fearful, and a bell-hammer stretched out to infinity was about to strike the last hour of Time, and split the universe asunder, when I awoke.

My soul wept for joy that it could again worship God ; and the joy, and the tears, and the belief in him, were the prayer. And when I arose the sun gleamed deeply behind the full purple ears of corn, and peacefully threw the reflection of its evening blushes on the little moon, which was rising in the east

Enoch walked with God.

without an aurora. And between the heavens and the earth a glad, fleeting world stretched out its short wings and lived like myself in the presence of the Infinite Father, and from all nature around us flowed sweet, peaceful tones, as from evening bells."[84]

REMEMBER.

With a Christian, at the end of a grievous trial, and when the soreness of it is abating, there is a strange and sublime experience. There is the feeling of sorrow, and there is that of infinite goodness, and the two blend into a consciousness like that of having been just about to be spoken to by God. And this is not a deceptive feeling, though God is silent towards us all our lives; for with him a thousand years are as one day; and when he will justify himself to us, it will not be our fleshly impatience which he will address, but the calm estate of spirits everlasting like himself."[86]

>Angel of Patience! sent to calm
>Our feverish brows with cooling palm;
>To lay the storms of hope and fear,
>And reconcile life's smile and tear;
>The throbs of wounded pride to still,
>And make our own our Father's will.
>
>O thou, who mournest on thy way,
>With longings for the close of day,

The Lord is at hand.

> He walks with thee, that angel kind,
> And gently whispers: "Be resigned,
> Bear up, bear on; the end shall tell,
> The dear Lord ordereth all things well!"⁵

I think, says Henry Ward Beecher, that the wickedest people on earth are those who use a force of genius to make themselves selfish in the noblest things; keeping themselves aloof from the vulgar and the ignorant and the unknown; rising higher and higher in taste, until they sit, ice upon ice, on the mountain-top of eternal congelation. Now, as we ascend the hills of improvement, those who are poor and needy are not to hear our voices chanting ever farther and farther in the distance. No! by our singing we are to win others upward to the same heights to which we aspire.

> We ask for peace, O Lord!
>   Thy children ask thy peace;
> Not what the world calls rest,
>   That toil and care should cease,
> That through bright sunny hours
>   Calm life should fleet away,
> And tranquil night should fade
>   In smiling day, —
> It is not for such peace that we would pray.
>
> It is thine own, O Lord!
>   Who toil while others sleep,

Come unto me, all ye that labor and are heavy laden.

>Who sow with loving care
> What other hands shall reap;
> They lean on thee, entranced,
> In calm and perfect rest;
> Give us that peace, O Lord!
> Divine and blest,
> Thou keepest for those hearts who love thee best.[151]

REMEMBER,

As opposed to passion, changefulness, or laborious exertion, repose is the especial and separating characteristic of the eternal mind and power; it is the "I am" of the Creator opposed to the "I become" of all creatures; it is the sign alike of the supreme knowledge which is incapable of surprise, the supreme power which is incapable of labor, the supreme volition which is incapable of change; it is the stillness of the beams of the eternal chambers laid upon the variable waters of ministering creatures; and as we see that the infinity which is a type of the Divine nature becomes yet more desirable from its peculiar address to our prison hopes, and to the expectations of an unsatisfied and unaccomplished existence, so the types of this attribute of the Deity seem to have been rendered further attractive to mortal instinct through the infliction upon the fallen creature of a curse neces-

ANGEL VOICES. 165

I will give you rest.

sitating a labor once unnatural and still most painful, so that the desire of rest planted in the heart is no sensual nor unworthy one, but a longing for renovation, and for escape from a state whose every phase is mere preparation for another equally transitory, to one in which permanence shall have become possible through perfection. Hence the great call of Christ to men, that call on which Saint Augustine fixed essential expression of Christian hope, is accompanied by the promise of rest, and the death bequest of Christ to men is peace.

As unity demanded for its expression what at first might have seemed its opposite, variety, so repose demands for its expression the implied capability of its opposite, energy. It is the most unfailing test of beauty: nothing can be ignoble that possesses it, nothing right that has it not.[81]

> He that lacks time to mourn lacks time to mend;
> Eternity mourns that. 'T is an ill cure
> For life's worst ills, to have no time to feel them.
> Where sorrow is held intrusive, and turned out,
> There wisdom will not enter, nor true power,
> Nor aught that dignifies humanity.[50]

REMEMBER.

Life is short. "Man has two minutes and

A time for every purpose, — a time to die.

a half to live, — one to smile, one to sigh, and a half to love; for in the middle of this he dies! But the grave is not deep: it is the shining tread of an angel that seeks us. When the unknown hand throws the fatal dart at the end of man, then boweth he his head, and the dart only lifts the crown of thorns from his wounds."[34]

> The time of life is short;
> To spend that shortness basely were too long,
> If Life did ride upon a dial's point,
> Still ending at the arrival of an hour.[50]

> "Leaves have their time to fall,
> And flowers to wither at the north-wind's breath,
> And stars to set: but all,
> Thou hast all seasons for thine own, O Death!"

REMEMBER.

It is not well for us to live in the constant atmosphere and presence of death; that would unfit us for life; but it is well for us, now and then, to talk with death as friend talketh with friend, and to bathe in the strange seas, and to anticipate the experiences of that land to which it will lead us. . . . . . Our spiritual life decays in the confinement and darkness of the world; and that it may gain new vigor, our thoughts must now and

Thy will be done.

then be unfurled and held high, and shaken in the air of heaven."⁵

REMEMBER,

The body is a more expert dialectician than the soul, and buffets it, even to bewilderment, with the empty bladders of logic; but the soul can retire from the dust and turmoil of such conflict, to the high tower of instinctive faith, and there, in hushed serenity, take comfort of the sympathizing stars. We look at death through the cheap glazed windows of the flesh, and believe him for the monster which the flawed and crooked glass presents him."

> "Choice befits not our condition :
> Acquiescence is the best."

> Complain not that the way is long :
>   What road is weary that leads there ?
> But let the angel take thy hand,
>   And lead thee up the misty stair ;
> And then with beating heart await
> The opening of the Golden Gate.

REMEMBER,

A trustful heart strengthens to the last. And to the last we will trust...... With us spring and summer and autumn and winter shall be the will of God ; and the will of God

Whosoever is born of God overcometh the world.

shall be the wisdom of the starry courses. The vital nature of the air about us shall be the will of God; and it shall be the will of God that we breathe without thinking. And to us joys shall be the will of God, and so shall pains and sorrows be. . . . . . And no less than birth, death shall be His will; and in it we will rejoice always, though sometimes, perhaps, not without trembling.[80]

REMEMBER,

There is nothing strictly immortal but immortality. Whatever hath no beginning, may be confident of no end: which is the peculiar of that necessary essence that cannot destroy itself, and the highest strain of omnipotency, to be so powerfully constituted as not to suffer even from the power of itself. . . . . . God, who can only destroy our souls, and hath assured our resurrection, either of our bodies or names, hath directly promised no duration. Wherein there is so much of chance that the boldest expectants have found unhappy frustration, and to hold long subsistence seems but a scope in oblivion. But man is a noble animal, splendid in ashes, and pompous in the grave, solemnizing nativities and deaths with

Many that sleep in the dust shall awake.

equal lustre, nor omitting ceremonies of bravery in the infancy of his nature.[18]

> So may we our lives control,
> Cast aside what we desire,
> Feeling that the sweeping soul
> Has than earthly path a higher.
>
> Life has bridged our destiny,
> Walled our woes within its breast,
> Runs through us a troubled sea
> Which perceiveth here no rest.
>
> Death shall sweep the works away,
> Set our current flowing free,
> Leave us no more yesterday,
> And be the thing we feebly see.[132]

REMEMBER,

The shore of the beautiful spring is steep, and we swim on the dead sea of life near the shore, but we the ephemera have no wings. Death, this sublime evening-red of our St. Thomas's day, this great amen of our hope, shouted across from yonder shore, would appear before our low couch like a beautiful crowned giant, and lift us up by degrees into the ether, and rock us there, were it not we are broken and stupefied ere thrown into his gigantic arms. It is illness alone that takes from death his glory; and the pinions of the aspiring soul (laden and stained with blood,

There shall be no more death nor sorrow.

tears, and clumps of earth) trail broken on the ground. But death is a flight, and no fall, only *then* when the hero throws himself upon one single fatal wound, and man stands like a spring-world full of new blossoms and old fruit, and the earth passes by him like a comet.[34]

> "So may we live, that every hour
> May die as dies the natural flower,
> A self-reviving thing of power;
> That every thought and every deed
> May hold within itself the seed
> Of future good and future meed."

> O Death! thou art the palace of our hopes,
> The storehouse of our joys, great labor's end,
> Thou art the bronzèd key which swiftly opes
> The coffers of the past: . . . . .
> Look not upon us till we chasten pride,
> And preparation make for thy high home;
> . . . . .
> I come, I come, think not I turn away!
> Fold round me thy gray robe! I stand to feel
> The setting of my last frail earthly day;
> I will not pluck it off, but calmly kneel:
> For I am great as thou art, though not thou,
> And thought as with thee dwells upon my brow.[132]

REMEMBER.

Pious spirits, who passed their days in raptures of futurity, made little more of this world than the world that was before it, while they lay obscure in the chaos of pre-ordina-

The sting of death is sin.

tion and night of their fore-beings. And if any have been so happy as truly to understand Christian annihilation, ectasis, exolution, liquefaction, transformation, the kiss of the spouse, gustation of God, and ingression into the Divine shadow, they have already had a handsome anticipation of heaven; the glory of the world is surely over and the earth in ashes unto them.[18]

> O fair! O fortunate! O rich! O dear!
> O happy, and thrice happy she,
> Dear silver-breasted dove,
>   Whoe'er she be,
>   Whose early love,
>   With wingèd vows,
> Makes haste to meet her morning spouse,
> And close with his immortal kisses.[100]

Life's harvest reap, like the wheat's fruitful ear.[e]

Remember.

Joy, most of all, loves to see Death at her festive board; for he is himself a joy, and the last rapture of earth. Only the vulgar can confound the heavenward soaring flight of humanity into the far land of the spring, with the mock funeral phenomena on the earth; in the same manner as they take the hooting of owls, on their departure for warmer climes, for the rattling of ghosts.[34]

> As the tree
> Stands in the sun, and shadows all beneath,
> So, in the light of great Eternity,
> Life *eminent* creates the shade of death;
> The shadow passeth when the tree shall fall,
> But life shall reign forever over all.[4]

He gave her therewith a sure token that he was a true messenger, and was come to bid her make haste to be gone. The token was an arrow, sharpened with love, let easily into her heart;—so Christiana knew that her time was come.

> We grieve not for those going,
> Their home and ours to find;
> For us our tears are flowing,
> For us who stay behind.
>
> Not those who 're havened yonder,
> Where rest and plenty bless;
> But we mourn those who wander
> Still in the wilderness.[24]

RESURRECTION.

"We awake and remember and understand."

Ich sag 'es jedem dass er lebt
Und auferstanden ist
Dass er im unserer Mitte schwebt
Und ewig bei uns ist. — *Novalis.*

He pleased God, and was beloved of him: so that, whereas he lived among sinners, he translated him. — *Wisdom of Solomon*, iv. 10.

Unto her is Paradise opened. — *Esdras.*

REMEMBER the words of St. Augustine: —

And *there*, in Abraham's bosom, whatever it be which that bosom signifies, lives my sweet friend. For what other place is there for such a soul?

O, Bearer of the key
That shuts and opens with a sound so sweet
Its turning in the wards is melody,
All things we move among are incomplete
And vain until we fashion them in Thee!

He is not here, he is risen.

Remember,

Resurrection is not one of those questions on which you can afford to wait; it is the question of life and death. There are times when it does not weigh heavily...... But at last a time comes when we feel it will be all over soon,—that much of our time is gone, and the rest swiftly going. And let a man be as frivolous as he will at heart, it is a question too solemn to be set aside,—whether he is going down into extinction and the blank of everlasting silence, or not...... Whether that thrilling, loving, thinking something that he calls himself has indeed within it an indestructible existence, which shall still be conscious when everything else shall have rushed into endless wreck. Oh! in the awful earnestness of a question such as that, a peradventure and a speculation will not do: we must have proof. The honest doubt of Thomas craves a sign as much as the cold doubt of the Sadducee. And a sign shall be mercifully given to the doubt of love which is refused to the doubt of indifference.

The Bible tells us of two kinds of proof of a Resurrection. The first is the evidence of the senses: "Thomas, because thou hast

The dead are raised up.

seen me, thou hast believed." The other is the evidence of the spirit: "Blessed are they that have not seen, and yet have believed."

The feeling which arose in the mind of Thomas, Christ pronounced to be faith: "Thomas, because thou hast *seen*, thou hast believed." ..... It matters not *how* faith comes, — whether God has many ways of bringing different characters thitherward; but that blessed thing which the Bible calls faith is a *state* of the soul, in which the things of God become glorious certainties.

There are men in whom the resurrection *begun* makes the resurrection credible. In them the spirit of the risen Saviour works already, and they have mounted with him from the grave. They have risen out of the darkness of doubt, and are expatiating in the brightness and sunshine of a day in which God is ever light."[147]

>   Hear what God, the Lord, hath spoken:
>   O my people, faint and few,
>   Comfortless, afflicted, broken,
>   Fair abodes I build for you;
>   Scenes of heart-felt tribulation
>   Shall no more perplex your ways;
>   You shall name your walls Salvation,
>   And your gates shall all be Praise.[152]

With what body do they come.

Remember,

I have drunk at many a fountain, but thirst came again; I have fed at many a bounteous table, but hunger returned; I have seen many bright and lovely things, but while I gazed, their lustre faded. There is nothing here that can give me rest; but when I behold thee, O God, I shall be satisfied![145]

> The golden palace of my God
> Towering above the clouds I see;
> Beyond the cherub's bright abode,
> Higher than angels' thoughts can be.
> How can I in those courts appear,
> Without a wedding-garment on?
> Conduct me, thou Life-giver, there,
> Conduct me to thy glorious throne!
> And clothe me with thy robes of light,
> And lead me through sin's darksome night,
>   My Saviour and my God.[153]

Remember,

Though this poor instrument, the human body, may be broken, the dial-plate effaced, and though the hidden artist can make no more signs, he may be rich as ever in the things to be signified. Fever may fire the pulses of the body; but wisdom and sanctity cannot sicken, be inflamed, and die. This would be to set the cross above the Crucified.[80]

ANGEL VOICES.

That which thou sowest is not quickened except it die.

One by one, we miss the voices which we loved so well to hear,
One by one, the kindly faces in the shadow disappear.

. . . . .

One whose feet the thorns have wounded passed that barrier, and came back
With a glory on his footsteps lighting yet the dreary track.
Boldly enter where he entered. All that seems but darkness here,
When thou once hast passed beyond it, haply shall be crystal clear.[85]

REMEMBER,

To subsist in lasting monuments, to live in their productions, to exist in their names and predicament of chimeras, was large satisfaction unto old expectations, and made one part of their Elysium. But all this is nothing in the metaphysics of true belief. To live indeed, is to be again ourselves, which being not only a hope but an evidence in noble believers, 't is all one to lie in St. Innocent's Churchyard as in the sands of Egypt, ready to be anything, in the ecstasy of being ever, and as content with six feet as the moles of Adrianus.[18]

> We saw Thee in thy balmy rest,
> Young dawn of our eternal day,
> We saw thine eyes break from the East,
> And chase the trembling shades away :
> We saw Thee and we blest the sight,
> We saw Thee by thine own sweet light.[13]

The glory of the celestial.

REMEMBER,

The world by wisdom knew not God; . . . . . but if obedience were entire and love were perfect, then would the revelation of the Spirit to the soul of men be perfect too; . . . . . every sight would be resplendent with beauty, and every sound would echo harmony; things common would become transfigured, as when the ecstatic state of the inward soul reflected a radiant cloud from the frame of Christ. The human would become Divine, — life, even the meanest, noble. In the hue of every violet there would be a glimpse of Divine affection and a dream of heaven. The forest would blaze with Deity, as it did to the eye of Moses. The creations of genius would breathe less of earth and more of heaven. Human love itself would burn with a clearer and intenser flame, rising from the altar of self-sacrifice.

These are "the things which God hath prepared for them that love him." Compared with these, what are loveliness, — the eloquent utterances of men, — the conceptions of the heart of Genius? What are they all to the serene stillness of a spirit lost in Love, — the full, deep rapture of a soul into which the

It is raised in power.

Spirit of God is pouring itself in a mighty tide of revelation?[147]

> Let them immortal wake
> Among the breathless flowers of Paradise,
> Where angel-songs of welcome with surprise
> This their last sleep may break,
> And to celestial joy their kindred souls invite.[154]

Remember,

The day of our decease will be that of our coming of age; and with our last breath we shall become free of the universe. And in some region of infinity, and from among its splendors, this earth will be looked back on like a lowly home, and this life of ours be remembered like a short apprenticeship to Duty.[86]

Remember,

This is the prerogative of noble natures, — that their departure to higher regions exercises a no less blessed influence than did their abode on earth; that they lighten us from above like stars, by which to steer our course, often interrupted by storms.[9]

> Deep, deep are loving eyes,
> Flowed with naphtha fiery sweet;
> And the point is paradise
> Where their glances meet;

Be ye therefore perfect.

Their reach shall yet be more profound,
And a vision without bound;

. . . . .

Higher far,
Upward unto the pure realm,
Over sun and star,
Over the flickering Dæmon film,
Thou must mount for love;

. . . . .

Where good and ill,
And joy and moan,
Melt into one.

. . . . .

Pray for a beam
Out of that sphere,
Thee to guide and to redeem.[15]

REMEMBER.

Three months' sunshine and rain have fostered out of dead earth all yonder beauty and abundance; but rain and sunshine, — what are they as agents, compared with holy influences like those which the Father Almighty can exert upon men's souls! Oh! there are persons whom we have known, whose spirits, divested of the numbing investiture of the flesh, they in God, and God in them, — concerning whom no magnitude of glory would seem incredible.[86]

O heavenly child of mortal birth!
Our thoughts of thee arise,
Not as a denizen of earth,
But inmate of the skies;

We shall bear the image of the heavenly.

To feel that life renewed is thine,
    A soothing balm imparts ;
We quaff from out Faith's cup divine,
    And Sabbath fills our hearts.

Thou leanest where the fadeless wands
    Of amaranth bend o'er ;
Thy white wings brush the golden sands
    Of Heaven's refulgent shore.
Thy home is where the psalm and song
    Of angels choir abroad ;
And blessed spirits all day long
    Bask round the throne of God.

REMEMBER,

This, the soul's questioning: If the soul lose this poor mansion of hers by the sudden conflagration of disease, or by the slow decay of age, is she therefore houseless and shelterless? If she cast away this soiled and tattered garment, is she therefore naked?—A child looks forward to his new suit, and dons it joyfully; we cling to our rags and foulness. Ask thyself, why we should not welcome Death as one who brings us tidings of the finding of long-lost titles to a large family estate, and set out gladly to take possession, though, it may be, not without a natural tear for the humbler home we are leaving. Death always means us a kindness, though he has often a gruff way of offering it. Even if the

Faith is the substance of things hoped for,

soul never returns from that chartless and unmapped country, which I do not believe, I would take this reason as a good one.[12]

> Farewell, brave relics of a complete man,
> Look up and see thy spirit made a star,
> . . . . . and, when thou sett'st
> Thy radiant forehead in the firmament,
> · Make the vast crystal crack with thy receipt,
> Spread to a world of fire, and the aged sky
> Cheer with new sparks of old humanity.[100]

'T is immortality to die aspiring.[100]

REMEMBER,

Nothing ever led man on to real victory but faith. . . . . . Even in this life he is a greater man, a man of more elevated character, who is steadily pursuing a plan that requires some years to accomplish, than he who is living by the day. Look forward but ten years, and plan for it, live for it; there is something of manhood, something of courage, required to conquer the thousand things that stand in your way. And therefore it is, that faith, and nothing but faith, gives victory in death. It is that elevation of character which we get from looking steadily and forever forward, till eternity becomes a real home to us, that enables us to look down upon the last

The evidence of things not seen.

struggle, and the funeral, and the grave, not as the great end of all, but only as something that stands between us and the end. We are conquerors of death when we are able to look beyond it.[147]

O Lord! by thee doth man live, and from thee is the life of my spirit; therefore wilt thou recover me, and make me to live!

> The steps of faith
> Fall on the seeming void, and find
> The rock beneath.[6]

Remember.

Even as God is the strength of the world, and the pervading presence of its glorious scenery, and of its plenteousness in field and meadows, valley, plain, and vineyard, and in stream and ocean, — so is the idea of God the strength of the soul: it is vast, quickening, congenial, satisfying; and under its influence legions of haunting imaginations, and besetting hosts of afflictive feelings, are put to flight, superseded in their place by warmth and gladness and freedom.[86]

> Blessed are they who see, and yet believe not,
> Yea, blest are they who look on graves, and still
> Believe none dead; who see proud tyrants ruling,
> And yet believe not in the strength of Evil, —

We shall all be changed.

Blessed are they who see the wandering poor,
And yet believe not that their God forsakes them;
Who see the blind worm creeping, yet believe not
That even that is left without a path.[158]

Remember,

Thou mourner for the dead! often dost thou go sorrowing after thy virtuous friend into the churchyard; but he is not there, for he is risen,—a spirit now among the just made perfect. In his coffin there are only grave-clothes and a decaying body, which, indeed, when living, was never more than a garment of earth. Be thou tranquil, since, in place of a worn-out body, thy lost companion is now clothed upon with immortality! . . . . . Look on the newly-made graves and see on them how the flowers spring more luxuriantly than before. So ought thy hopes to rise up the more strongly out of sorrow; and not only to spring up on high, but also to blossom there, and ripen those consolatory fruits which drop down into the soul, like manna from heaven.[86]

> Well done of God to halve the lot,
> And give her all the sweetness;
> To us, the empty room and cot;
> To her, the heaven's completeness.

ANGEL VOICES.   185

The living, the living, he shall praise thee.

    To us the grave ; to her the rows
        The mystic palm-trees spring in ;
    To us, the silence in the house ;
        To her, the choral singing !

    Grow fast in heaven, sweet Lily clipped,
        In love more calm than this is ;
    And may the angels, dewy lipped,
        Remind thee of our kisses !

    While none shall tell thee of our tears,
        These human tears now falling,
    Till, after a few patient years,
        One home shall take us all in.[150]

REMEMBER.

There is an inner *heart*-contained spirit-world, which breaks through the dark clouds of the body-world as a warm sun. I mean the inner universe of virtue, beauty, and truth ; three soul-worlds and heavens, which are neither parts nor shoots nor cuttings nor copies of the outer one. ...... This inner universe, which is still more glorious and admirable than the outer, needs another heaven than the one above us, and a higher world than one a sun now shines upon. Therefore we rightly say, not a second earth or globe, but a second *world*, — another beyond the universe.[34]

Remember the words of Professor Nichol, who, drawing us reverently after him, to gaze upon the unspeakable glories of the heavens,

The heavens declare thy glory.

compared with whose light all knowledge is but as the faintest star, says: "Grand thoughts and deeds, as well as physical marvels, spring up without apparent parentage in our world; but angelic natures penetrate to their birthplace, and by the sight are strengthened still further to adore...... In the vast heavens, as well as among phenomena around us, all things are in a state of change and progress; here too, — on the sky, — in splendid hieroglyphics, the truth is inscribed, that the grandest forms of present being are only germs, swelling and bursting with a life to come! And if the universal fabric is thus fixed and constructed, shall aught that it contains be un-upheld by the same preserving law? is annihilation a possibility, real or virtual, — the stoppage of the career of any advancing being, while *Hospitable Infinitude remains?* No! let the night fall: it prepares a dawn when man's weariness shall have ceased, and his soul be refreshed and restored. *To come!* To every creature these are words of hope spoken in organ tones: our hearts suggest them, and the stars repeat them, and through the Infinite, aspiration wings its way, rejoicingly, as an eagle follows the sun."

ANGEL VOICES. 187

Where your treasure is, there will your heart be also.

REMEMBER,

When engineers would bridge a stream, they often carry over at first but a single cord. With that, next, they stretch a wire across. Then strand is added to strand, until a foundation is laid for planks; and now the bold engineer finds safe footway, and walks from side to side. So God takes from us some golden-threaded pleasure, and stretches it thence to heaven. Then he takes a child, and then a friend. Thus he bridges death, and teaches the thoughts of the most timid to find their way hither and thither between the shores.[145]

> 'T is but one family, — the accents come
> Like light from heaven to break the night of woe,
> The banner cry to call the spirit home,
> The shout of victory o'er a fallen foe.
>
> Death never separates; the golden wires,
> That ever trembled to their names before,
> Will vibrate still, though every form expires,
> And those we love we look upon no more.
>
> No more indeed in sorrow and in pain,
> But even memory's need erelong will cease,
> For we shall join the lost of love again,
> In endless bands, and in eternal peace.[159]

And remember, neither the day nor the

The master calleth for thee.

hour knoweth any man. "In the very middle of Spenser's great work he was called"; and the lines that happened to be the last from his pen are as though they had been meant against his death :—

> For all that moveth doth in change delight,
> But thenceforth all shall rest eternally
> With Him that is the God of Sabaoth hight;
> O, that great Sabaoth God, grant me that Sabbath's sight.

. . . . . Of this poet's having died, I do not think. And it is as though Spenser had been changed while talking with me. And then I think how, to the angels, this whole earth looks like a Mount of Transfiguration. . . . . . We hear a poet singing; and while we listen, we are bettered, and silent, we are enraptured. Then while we are listening so eagerly, the voice dies away into silence and into heaven. . . . . . Celestial was the last word Keats wrote, and then he himself became it.[80]

> Ah! what time wilt thou come? when shall that crie,
> The Bridegroome's comming! fill the sky?
> Shall it in the evening run,
> When our words and works are done?
> Or will thy all-surprizing light
>   Break at midnight,
> When either sleep, or some dark pleasure
> Possesseth mad man without measure?

Who maketh his angels spirits.

> Or shall these early, fragrant hours
> Unlock thy bowers,
> And with their blush of light descry,
> Thy locks crown'd with eternitie?"

Remember,

Although we are accustomed to think of heaven as distant, of this we have no proof. Heaven is the union, the society, of spiritual, higher beings. May not these fill the universe? Milton has said,

> "Millions of spiritual beings walk the earth,
> Both when we wake and when we sleep."

A new sense, a new eye, might show the spiritual world compassing us on every side. Whilst we know not to what place our friends go, we know what is infinitely more interesting, to what beings they go. We know not where heaven is, but we know whom it contains; and this knowledge opens to us an infinite field for contemplation and delight. They who are born into heaven go not only to Jesus, and an innumerable company of pure beings; they go to God. These new relations of the ascended spirit to the Universal Father, how near! how tender! how strong! how exalting! But this is too great a subject for the space which remains; and

All that are in the graves shall hear his voice.

yet is it the chief element of the felicity of heaven.[155]

"Come away! above the storm
Ever shines the blue;
Come away! beyond the form
Ever lies the true."

Every man I part with is a soul to be met again, and every face I see is what will be bright with the light of heaven some time, and in my sight. Duty reaches down ages in its effects, and into eternity...... Every day the world is ripening against that harvest which is to be at the end of it; slowly perhaps; and yet not so very slowly, considering what the fruits of it are to be, for they will be eternal, they will be souls, — everlasting souls.[86]

In some hour of solemn jubilee
The massy gates of Paradise are thrown
Wide open, and forth come, in fragments wild,
Sweet echoes of unearthly melodies,
And odors snatched from beds of amaranth,
And they that from the crystal river of life
Spring up on freshened wing, ambrosial gales!
The favored good man in his lonely walk
Perceives them, and his silent spirit drinks
Strange bliss, which he shall recognize in heaven.[19]

That we, with sin polluted,
Should have our home so high!
That we should dwell in mansions
Beyond the starry sky!

Father, I will that they be with me where I am.

> And now we fight the battle,
> And then we wear the crown
> Of full and everlasting
> And ever bright renown.[105]

REMEMBER,

Faith, Hope, and Love, these three, but the greatest of these is Love...... And in that there is all comfort for them that hope to meet again...... O, if there is a heaven for our faith, there are friends in it for our love. I have known those who have grown holy through thoughts of the dead. I have known one who, as he prayed, always felt, as it were, the presence of a spirit about him, — one of the blessed vanished. And it was in her spirit he prayed, and was earnest in prayer. Another person I have known, to whom the meeting of her husband was all of heaven, beside God; for he had been the husband of her soul, as well as her youth, and they had suffered much together, but she much more by herself. We are saved by hope, and some of us by the special hope of being with our friends again. So that if there is salvation by hope, our friends whom we so hope for we shall certainly have again.[86]

Transition into the divine is ever woful, yet it is life. — *Bettina.*

Jesus said, I am the resurrection and the life.

They who die in Christ are blessed, —
    Ours be, then, no thought of grieving!
Sweetly with their God they rest,
    All their toils and troubles leaving.
So be ours the faith that saveth,
Hope that every trial leaveth,
Love that to the end endureth,
And through Christ the crown secureth. [161]

To Death's dark land some heedless go;
    But there was One
Who searched it quite through to and fro,
And then, returning like the sun,
Discovered all that there is done.

And since his death we throughly see
    All the dark way;
Those shades but thin and narrow be,
Which his first looks will quickly fray;
Mists make but triumphs for the day. [54]

REMEMBER.

When man finds that if he would do God's will, however imperfectly, he must offer up this continual sacrifice, *the sacrifice of his own will,* his thoughts are irresistibly carried to rest upon that one offering up of a higher than any human will, by which Christ has perfected forever them that are sanctified.

The more deeply we feel the existing contradiction between God's will and that of his creature, the deeper becomes our sense of the need of somewhat to take it away, so that the

The communion of saints.

heart draws near to a truth unapproachable by the intellect, — *the necessary death of Christ.* All things in nature, as well as all things in grace, point to a Redeemer. Nature struggles, but she cannot speak; she remains in bondage with her children, dumb like them, and beautiful. Humanity has found a voice, but where, save for Christ, would she find an answer? She has showed him of her wound, her grievous, incurable hurt, and how has he consoled her? Even by showing her his, — "Reach hither thy hand, and thrust it into my side."[58]

REMEMBER.
Unto you is paradise opened, the tree of life is planted, the time to come is prepared, plenteousness is ready, a city is builded, and rest is allowed, yea, perfect goodness and wisdom.

Remember, Soul! out of this straitened and fiery place thou shalt escape, —

And thou shalt walk in soft, white light, with kings and priests abroad,
And thou shalt summer high in bliss upon the hills of God.[162]

REMEMBER.
The Divinity is already very near to that

As he lay and slept, an angel touched him.

man who has succeeded in collecting all beauty and greatness, all excellence, both in the small and great of nature, and in evolving from this manifoldness the great unity. The whole creation sinks into his personality. If each man loved all men, then every individual would possess the world."[39]

Remember

The vision of Dante, who, seeing the birds as they flew, fall dead, questioned of that fantasy. Then one answered him, "Dost thou not know? Thy wondrous lady has departed from this world." "I began," said Dante, "to weep very piteously, and wept not only in imagination, but with my eyes, bathing them with real tears. Then I imagined that I looked toward heaven, and it seemed to me that I saw a multitude of angels who were returning upwards, having before them a little cloud of exceeding whiteness. It seemed to me that these angels sang gloriously, and that the words of their song were these: 'Osanna in Excelsis!' and other than these I did not hear.

"Then the heart in which abode such great love seemed to say to me, 'True is it that our lady lieth dead.' And thereupon I seemed to

God is a spirit.

go to behold that body in which that most noble and blessed soul had been. And the erring fancy was so strong that it showed to me this lady dead, and it appeared to me that ladies were covering her head with a white veil, and that her face had such an aspect of humility that it seemed to say, 'I behold the beginning of peace.'"[163]

> Pure, meek, with soul serene,
> Sweeter it was to her to serve unseen
> Her God, than reign a queen.
>
> Now far above our sight,
> Enthroned upon the azure star-paved height,
> She reigns in realms of light;
>
> So long as time shall flow
> Teaching to all who sit on thrones below,
> The good that power can do.[146]

REMEMBER,

The joys of heaven are spiritual. The fleshly-minded think more of the chrysolites, the amethysts, the sapphires, with which the city of God is resplendent, than even of the Son of God, who is himself the chief glory of that house not made with hands; just as their Jewish predecessors esteemed Christ's miracles more than his Messiahship, and the

Ye also, as lively stones, are built up, a spiritual house.

twelve baskets' full of meat more than that spirit which was given to Jesus without measure. So they be of a purifying tendency, and spiritual in character, our hopes, then, cannot be too vast to be Christian. Eternity is the divine treasure-house, and hope is the window, by means of which mortals are permitted to see, as through a glass darkly, the things which God is preparing.[80]

> He saw through life and death, through good and ill,
>   He saw through his own soul.
> The marvel of the everlasting will,
>   An open scroll,
>   Before him lay.[4]

Remember.

It is impossible to be a hero in anything, unless one is first a hero in faith.[104]

Remember.

In claiming a *personal* relation with God, nothing *exclusive* is intended; nay, he who thus learns he is loved by God, learns simultaneously that all other men and creatures are also loved. That is an important lesson for the man's external action, — indeed, is a foundation of universal love in the soul; but its inward movements towards God proceed

By faith Enoch was translated, that he should not see death.

exactly as if there were no other creatures beside itself in the universe. Thus the discovery that *it loves* and *is loved in turn*, produces sensible joy; in some natures very powerful, in all imparting cheerfulness, hope, vivacity. The personal relation sought is discerned and felt. The soul understands and knows that God is *her* God, dwelling with her more closely than any creature can. Yea, neither stars nor sea nor smiling Nature hold God so intimately as the bosom of the soul. It no longer seems profane to say, "God is my bosom friend; God is for me, and I am for him." So joy bursts into praise, and all things look brilliant; and hardship seems easy, and duty becomes delight, and contempt is not felt, and every morsel of bread is sweet.[104]

> Death is upon me, yet I fear not now.
> Open my chamber window, — let me look
> Upon the sunny vales, the sunny glow
> That fills each alley, close, and copsewood nook.
> I know them, love them, mourn them not to leave;
> Existence and its change my spirit cannot grieve![105]

>   Let the king
> Me ever into these his cellars bring,
> Where flows such wine as we can have of none
> But Him who trod the wine-press all alone;

I am come that ye might have life.

> Wine of youth's life, and the sweet deaths of love;
> Wine of immortal mixture, which can prove
> Its tincture from the rosy nectar; wine
> That can exalt weak earth; and so refine
> Our dust, that at one draught mortality
> May drink itself up, and forget to die.[103]

REMEMBER the last words of Jean Paul:—

Life is not flown with the soul, but in the soul, which lays down its organic sceptre. The sceptre releases from its service the intellectual world which it had governed till now, or rather the intellectual world abandons it.

> When Faith and Love which parted from thee never
> Had ripened thy just soul to dwell with God,
> Meekly thou didst resign this earthly load
> Of death called life, which us from Life doth sever.[17]

Nations and men are only the *best* when they are the gladdest, and deserve Heaven when they enjoy it.[84]

> O purblind race of miserable men,
> How many among us at this very hour
> Do forge a lifelong trouble for ourselves,
> By taking true for false, or false for true;
> Here, through the feeble twilight of this world
> Groping, how many, until we pass and reach
> That other, where we see as we are seen![4]

I, if I be lifted up, will draw all men unto me.

My voice that long hath faltered, shall be still.
The mystic darkness drops from Calvary's hill
Into the common light of this day's sun.[130]

REMEMBER,

The prayer of persevering faith is a hymn of sacrifice; the sigh of sorrow that hopes is a chant of resignation, "the desire of the night for the morning," and the outgoing of charity is one prolonged canticle of love!

The voice that sings is the prayer of the world, — it is the morning hymn, announcing the awakening of the ages, as the song of birds heralds the opening of the day!

The martyrs sang amid their punishments, for the faith in their souls felt itself immortal, like the Phœnix, and resumed a new youth amid the flames of the stake. The poetry of the soul awakens harmonies in the last dying sighs of the just, and sings, like the swan of our fable, its passage to other realms of life.

Leave in tears those children of the earth who feel but present pain, nor dream of good to come. But you, children of heaven, poets of charity, of hope and faith, — you, who could see the world broken to pieces without ceasing to bless God in the midst of its ruins, prophet consolers, sing, sing ever.

I heard the voice of harpers harping with their harps:

Let us love, and the life of our hearts shall be a song-burst of goodness towards all ; for love is all harmony ; and if you ask me what is this Voice that sings, I will answer, It is the Voice of Love, the Believer."[106]

> O Thou Æternal banquet ! where
> Forever we
> May feed without satietie !
> Who harmonie art to the eare !
> Who art, while all things else appeare ! [107]

REMEMBER,

All the sweetest songs and the grandest and most touching poetry that have ever been on earth, breathed into sound or written in characters, have sprung out of work and strife, sorrow and peril. And why should not a new song, unknown even to the elder seraphs, be so composed and framed in heaven, out of all life's trouble and disaster, while the mercy of God, the atoning influence of Christ, all heavenly help and guidance that they have received in their struggles, shall add depth and melody to those voices of the redeemed ?[22]

> The light of her young life went down,
> As sinks behind the hill
> The glory of a setting star,
> Clear, suddenly, and still.

And they sung as it were a new song before the throne.

> As pure and sweet her fair brow seemed,
>   Eternal as the sky;
> And like the brook's low song her voice,
>   A sound which could not die.
>
> Sweet promptings unto kindest deeds
>   Were in her very look;
> We read her face as one who reads
>   A true and holy book.
>
> The measure of a blessed hymn,
>   To which our hearts could move;
> The breathing of an inward psalm,
>   A canticle of love.[5]

Remember,

Public calamity should not, as theologians assert, make us humble, but proud. When the long, heavy sword of war sinks down upon mankind, and when a thousand wan, cloven hearts bleed, — or when in the clear blue evening the smoking, hot cloud of a city thrown upon the funeral pile hangs darkly in the heavens, as it were the clouds of dust from a thousand hearts and joys, lying in ashes, — let the spirit proudly raise itself and loathe the tear, and that for which it falls, and let it say: "Thou art much too insignificant, common life, for the disconsolateness of an immortal, thou life, sent and deformed in the mass! — On this globe, rounded out of ashes

In thy presence is fulness of joy.

of thousands of years, under these earthly storms of mist, in this wailing of a dream, it is a shame that the sigh falls into dust only with its breast, and not sooner; and the tear only with its eye!"[34]

> The many waves of thought, the mighty tides,
>   The ground-swell that rolls up from other lands,
> From far-off worlds, from dim, eternal shores,
>   Whose echo dashes on life's way-worn strands, —
> This vague, dark tumult of the inner sea
> Grows calm, grows bright, O risen Lord, in thee!
>
> Thy piercèd hand guides the mysterious wheels;
>   Thy thorn-crowned brow now wears the crown of power;
> And when the dark enigma presseth sore,
>   Thy patient voice saith, "Watch with me one hour!"
> As sinks the moaning river in the sea,
> In silver peace, — so sinks my soul in Thee.[127]

REMEMBER.

The happy seasons when we may say, "My spirit raises itself to-day with all its earthly strength, — I lift up my eyes to the infinite world beyond this life, — my heart of dust, knit to a purer Fatherland, beats aloft to thy starry heavens, Thou Infinite Being, to the constellation of thy boundless form; and I became great and eternal through thy voice sounding in the inmost, noblest feelings of my nature, 'Thou shalt never perish.'"

At thy right hand there are pleasures forevermore.

Let him who with me recollects an hour when the angel of peace appeared to him, and drew beloved souls from his earthly embrace, — ah! let him who remembers an hour in which he lost too much, subdue his languishing, and with me look steadfastly to the clouds and say, "Repose continually on your clouds. Ye beloved ones who have been snatched away from us, ye number not the centuries that flow betwixt your evening and your morning; no stone lies any longer on your protected hearts, except the tombstone, — and that presses you not, — and never does a thought on us disturb your rest." . . . . .

Deep in man lies a something unconquerable, which sorrow only benumbs, but does not vanquish. Therefore it is that he supports a life, in which the best of us bear foliage only instead of fruits; therefore it is that he watches out almost the nights of this Western globe, wherein the objects of his best affections pass over his loving breast into a far-distant land; while, like swans that fly through Iceland's gloomy nights with tones of the violin, they leave behind to the present world only the after-sounds of pleasing recollections.[34]

Blessed are they which are called unto the marriage supper of the Lamb.

    Heaven is no flaming lustre, made of light;
       No sweet content, or well-tuned harmony;
    Ambrosia, for to feast the appetite;
       Or flowery odor mixed with spicery;
       No soft embrace or pleasure bodily.
    And yet it is a kind of inward feast,
    A harmony that sounds within the breast,
    An odor, light, embrace, in which the soul doth rest.

    A heavenly feast no hunger can consume;
       A light unseen, yet shines in every place;
    A sound no time can steal; a sweet perfume
       No winds can scatter; an entire embrace
       That no satiety can e'er unlace;
    Ingraced into so high a favor there,
    The saints with their beaupeers whole worlds outwear,
    And things unseen do see, and things unheard do hear.

    Ye blessed souls, grown richer by your spoil,
       Whose loss, though great, is cause
          Of greater gains;
    Here may your weary spirits rest from toil,
       Spending your endless evening that remains
       Among those white flocks and celestial trains
    That feed upon their Shepherd's eyes, and frame
    That heavenly music of so wondrous frame,
    Psalming aloud the holy honors of his name![168]

        Eternity! eternity!
        How long art thou, Eternity!
        A little bird with fretting beak
        Might wear to naught the loftiest peak,
        Though but each thousand years it came,
        Yet thou wert then, as now, the same.
        Ponder, O man, Eternity![118]

I will see you again, and your heart shall rejoice.

REMEMBER,

All that are in Christ must be made to drink into one Spirit; yet often, perhaps, must he return and ask his chosen ones, "Are ye able to drink of my cup?" before that free, calm answer can be given, "We are able"; and many offerings must be laid upon his altar with tears and weeping before the *sacrifices of joy* are brought there. For, as Christ was made like unto us, we must *be made like unto him*, even at the cost of much that is grievous to natural feeling. His coming within the soul is the bringing in of a new order; and when was there a painless transition, a bloodless revolution?

"They were all baptized in the cloud and in the sea"; this is the register of all Christ's chosen ones...... When the veil of the temple, even this poor worn garment of our Humanity, is rent from the top to the bottom, we catch glimpses of the inner glory: the rocks are riven, the graves open, they who have long slept in the dust come forth and reveal to us awful and tender secrets, of which otherwise we should have known nothing."

REMEMBER,

If only men's sighs lived on the air, we

Jesus Christ the same yesterday, to-day, and forever.

could not bear the sound. But it is as though God did hear what man would not bear to hear; for to his nature it is possible, and to his almightiness it would be endurable, and in the ear of his foreknowledge it would be a sublime sound; for as he listens from everlasting to everlasting, it is as though voices that are anguish one moment are crying aloud with all angels the next. But, indeed, with God, past, present, and future are one; and to his eyes, in the sowing of tears, there is ripe at once the golden harvest of joy.[66]

> I got me flowers to strew Thy way;
> I got me boughs off many a tree;
> But Thou wast up at break of day,
> And brought'st thy sweets along with Thee.
>
> The sun arising in the east,
> Though he give light, and the east perfume;
> If they should offer to contest
> With Thy arising, they presume.
>
> Can there be any day but this,
> Though many suns to shine endeavor?
> We count three hundred, but we miss:
> There is but one, and that one ever.[70]
>
> Wem Zeit ist wie die Ewigkeit
> Und Ewigkeit ist wie die Zeit
> Der est befreit von allem Streit.

The chariots of God are thousands of angels.

REMEMBER,

They are the chariots of His will, they bear His will about to every part of the universe. This is their delight. They bless God who vouchsafes thus to employ them. But when they have fulfilled God's message, then they return back to Him, and stand before Him drinking in fresh streams of life and strength and purity and joy from His presence."

> How oft do they their silver bowers leave,
> To come to succour us that succour want!
> How oft do they with golden pinions cleave
> The flitting skyes like flying pursuivant,
> Against fowle fiends to ayd us militant!
> They for us fight, they watch, and dewly ward,
> And their bright squadrons round about us plant,
> And all for love and nothing for reward;
> O why should heavenly God to men have such regard!²³

REMEMBER,

Great sufferers in this world are not very rare, and so are no wonder to us; but our human mysteries are mysteries to the angels, and things they desire to look into. Yet a good man's suffering must be the wonder of many a heavenly dweller; he having himself been formed through another discipline than that of endurance, perhaps...... And there are heavenly spirits, to whom the knowledge

> God shall wipe away all tears from their eyes.

of our righteous sufferers must be more prophetic of creative newness than a voice would be, if heard calling down the depths of infinity, to let new worlds be started. Yes, Paul, yes! Thy Lord and Master, and mine, — if we suffer with Him, we shall be also glorified together.[86]

  A host of angels flying,
   Through cloudless skies impelled,
   Upon the earth beheld
  A pearl of beauty lying,
   Worthy to glitter bright,
   In heaven's vast halls of light.

  They saw with glances tender
   An infant newly born,
   O'er whom life's earliest morn
  Just cast its opening splendor :
   Virtue it could not know,
   Nor vice, nor joy, nor woe.

  The blest angelic legion
   Greeted its birth above,
   And came, with looks of love,
  From heaven's enchanting region ;
   Bending their wingéd way
   To where the infant lay.

  They spread their pinions o'er it, —
   That little pearl which shone
   With lustre all its own, —
  And then on high they bore it,
   Where glory has its birth ;
   But left the shell on earth.[162]

He turneth the shadow of death into morning.

Love strong as death measures eternity.

Two worlds there are. To one our eyes we strain,
Whose magic joys we shall not see again ;
  Bright haze of morning veils its glimmering shore.
      Ah, truly breathed we there
        Intoxicating air, —
Glad were our hearts in that sweet realm of Nevermore.

Upon the frontier of this shadowy land
We, pilgrims of eternal sorrows, stand ;
  What realm lies forward, with its happier store
      Of forests green and deep,
      Of valleys hushed in sleep,
And lakes most peaceful ? 'T is the land of Evermore.

They whom we loved and lost so long ago
Dwell in those cities far from mortal woe, —
  Haunt those fresh woodlands, whence sweet carollings soar.
      Eternal peace have they :
      God wipes their tears away :
They drink that river of life which flows for Evermore.[170]

REMEMBER.

O man, take now this light of life, which was in the Word, and is eternal ; and behold the Being of all beings, and especially thyself : seeing thou art an image, life, and derive thy being of the unsearchable God ; and a likeness as to him. Here consider time and eternity ; heaven and hell ; this world ; light and darkness ; pain, and the source ; life and death. Here examine thyself, whether thou hast the light and life of the Word in thee; so shalt thou be able to see and understand all things; for thy life was in the Word, and was made manifest in the image which God created; it was breathed into it from the Spirit of the Word."

REMEMBER.

The heart accepts Christ because it needs him, even while the mind may be unable to receive him fully, because the orbit of this star is so extended as to carry it beyond the sphere of human intelligence. . . . . . Enough to learn that we shall find no higher thing above, shall pierce to no deeper thing below, than the cross and its solemn and tender teachings. If we would climb up into heaven, it is there; if we would go down into hell, it is there also. He alone among men who has clasped this great mystery of grief and love to his bosom sees, if it be as yet but through a glass darkly, how pain and love, yes, joy also, *all things that have a living root in humanity*, come to bloom under its shadow. And how love that cannot die, and faith that grows to certainty, and hope that maketh not

Seek out the glory for such as be like thee.

ashamed, root themselves about it with all fair things that wither in life, and noble things for which it has no room. "I took," said Luther, "for the symbol of my theology a seal on which I had engraven a cross with a heart in its centre; the cross is black, to indicate the sorrows, even unto death, through which the Christian must pass, *but the heart preserves its natural color*, for the cross does not extinguish nature, it does not kill, but gives life. *Justus fide vivet sed fide crucifixi.* The heart is placed in the midst of a white rose, which signifies the joy, peace, and consolation that faith gives; *but the rose is white, not red*, because it is not the joy and peace of the world, but that of spirits."

"Whoso is wise will ponder these things, and he shall understand the loving-kindness of the Lord.'"[66]

> They are all gone into the world of light!
> And I alone sit lingering here!
> Their very memory is fair and bright,
> And my sad thoughts doth clear.
>
> He that hath found some fledged bird's nest may know
> At first sight if the bird be flown;
> But what fair dell or grove he sings in now,
> That is to him unknown.[54]

The world passeth away, and the lusts thereof;

REMEMBER,

The withdrawal of a friend from our side is a special providence, even for ourselves. Never does the grave take hold of a mortal's feet, but his companion hath an omnipresent eye the while fixed on him in compassion. We should think of that eye, as well as of the hand that taketh away. Meditation on the dead quickens our faith in the unseen, for sorrow hath a sacred efficacy; there being no touch so purifying as that of a dead man's hand; and few living objects having such regenerative power as the sight of a fellow-mortal's death.[86]

>Virtue thus
>Sets forth and magnifies herself; thus feeds
>A calm, and beautiful, and silent fire,
>From the encumbrances of mortal life,
>From error, disappointment, nay, from guilt.[35]

Let us awake to righteousness! May Christ present us, one and all, faultless before God's throne! And at our solemn trial may all the earthly witness proffered be that of our good works, such as do follow the blessed dead that die in the Lord![86]

>Flowers gathered in this world die here; if thou
>Wouldst have a wreath that fades not, let them grow,
>And grow for thee. Who spares them here shall find
>A garland where comes neither rain nor wind.[54]

He that doeth the will of God abideth forever.

The best thing in being man, after all, is that the good which we have enjoyed does not perish from us, — that it establishes itself within and around us, propagates itself, multiplies; and that thus we acquire ever more power for greater enjoyment.[194]

    No more, in heaven no more
      That face a shadow bears,
    But looks of light, born of a bliss
      Unknown to earth, it wears.

    No more, in heaven no more
      That voice is faint with pain;
    It mingles with angelic bards,
      In their enraptured strain.

    No more, in heaven no more
      The parting grief is known;
    But love has all eternity
      To look through as its own.[172]

REMEMBER,

Man feels himself to be greater than the universe, yet feebler than the meanest thing within it which can follow the appointed law of its being. The splendor also of his material acquisitions is but a robe too short and thin to wrap him from cold and shame.[50]

They are not of the world, even as I am not of the world.

REMEMBER,

There is a sadness in all Idealism; it lifts the soul into a region where it cannot now dwell; it must return to earth, and it is hard for it not to do so at the shock of a keen revulsion, the dashing of the foot against a stone. But in no life does the secret of all tragedy, the conflict between the will and the circumstance, so unfold itself as in that of the Christian; he, of all men, feels and mourns over that sharp, ever-recurring contrast of our existence, — the glorious capabilities, the limited attainments, of man's nature and destiny below.[56]

> *World's use* is cold, *world's love* is vain,
> *World's cruelty* is bitter bane,
> But pain is not the fruit of pain.
>
> I am content to be so bare
> Before the archers, everywhere
> My wounds being stroked by heavenly air.[150]

REMEMBER.

The sphere of the soul is then luciform, when the soul is neither extended to anything (external), nor inwardly concurs with it, nor is depressed by it, but is illuminated with a light by which she sees the truth of all things, and the truth that is in herself.[175]

Whosoever will, let him come and drink of the water of life freely.

REMEMBER,

Between these two magnificent notes rolls the anthem of God's mercy. "Whosoever will"! That is the beginning and the ending. Let every Christian heart respond in those final and sublimest words of revelation, — "Even so, come, Lord Jesus!"[145]

REMEMBER

This experience, common, at an earlier or later age, to all humanity, and remember the mortal sorrow as an immortal blessedness. . . . . . Thou, around whose ample brow, as often as thy sweet countenance rises in the darkness, I fancy a tiara of light or a gleaming aureola in token of thy premature intellectual grandeur, ... thou too wert summoned away from our nursery; and the night which for me gathered upon that event ran after my steps far into life; and perhaps at this day I resemble little for good or for ill that which else I should have been. Pillar of fire that didst go before me to guide and to quicken, — pillar of darkness, when thy countenance was turned away to God, that didst too truly reveal to my dawning fears the secret shadow of death, — by what mysteri-

Unto him that is able to keep us from falling, and to present us

ous gravitation was it that my heart had been drawn to thine? Could a child six years old place any special value upon intellectual forwardness? . . . . . Hadst thou been an idiot, my sister, I must have loved thee, having that capacious heart! . . . . . This it was which crowned thee with beauty and power.

"Love, the holy sense,
Best gift of God, in thee was most intense."

. . . . . Rightly it is said of utter, utter misery, it "cannot be remembered." . . . . . On the day after my sister's death, whilst the sweet temple of her brain was yet unviolated by human scrutiny, I formed my own scheme for seeing her once more. . . . . . I imagine that it was about an hour after high noon when I reached the chamber door; it was locked, but the key was not taken away. Entering, I closed the door so softly that, although it opened upon a hall which ascended through all the stories, no echo ran along the silent walls. Then, turning round, I sought my sister's face. But the bed had been moved, and the back was now turned towards myself. Nothing met my eye but one large window, wide open, through which the sun of midsum-

faultless before the presence of his glory with his holy angels.

mer at midday was showering down torrents of splendor. The weather was dry, the sky was cloudless, the blue depths seemed the express types of infinity; and it was not possible for eye to behold or for heart to conceive any symbols more pathetic of life and the glory of life. . . . . . . From the gorgeous sunlight I turned around to the corpse. There lay the sweet, childish figure; there the angel face; and, as people usually fancy, it was said in the house that no features had suffered any change. Had they not? The forehead, indeed, the serene, noble forehead, — that might be the same; but the frozen eyelids, the darkness that seemed to steal from beneath them, the marble lips, the stiffening hands, laid palm to palm, as if repeating the supplications of closing anguish, — could these be mistaken for life? Had it been so, wherefore did I not spring to those heavenly lips with tears and never-ending kisses? But so it was *not*. I stood checked for a moment; awe, not fear, fell upon me; and, whilst I stood, a solemn wind began to blow, — the saddest that ear ever heard. It was a wind that might have swept the fields of mortality for a thousand centuries. Many times since, upon summer

To the only wise God be honor and glory.

days, when the sun is about the hottest, I have remarked the same wind arising, and uttering the same hollow, solemn, Memnonian, but saintly swell; it is in this world the one great *audible* symbol of eternity...... Grief! thou art classed among the depressing passions. And true it is that thou humblest to the dust, but also thou exaltest to the clouds. Thou shakest as with ague, but also thou steadiest as with frost. Thou sickenest the heart, but also thou healest its infirmities......

On Sunday mornings I went with the rest of my family to church; it was a church on the ancient model of England, having aisles, galleries, organ, all things ancient and venerable, and the proportions majestic. Here, whilst the congregation knelt through the long litany, as often as we came to that passage, so beautiful amongst many that are so, where God is supplicated on behalf of "all sick persons and young children," and that he would "show his pity upon all prisoners and captives," I wept in secret; and, raising my streaming eyes to the upper windows of the galleries, saw, on days when the sun was shining, a spectacle as affecting as ever prophet

To him that overcometh will I give to eat of the tree of life.

can have beheld. The *sides* of the windows were rich with storied glass; through the deep purples and crimsons streamed the golden light; emblazonries of heavenly illuminations (from the sun) mingling with the earthly emblazonries (from art and its gorgeous coloring) of what is grandest in man. *There* were the apostles that had trampled upon earth and the glories of earth, out of celestial love to man. *There* were the martyrs that had borne witness to the truth through flames, through torments, and through armies of fierce, insulting faces. . . . . . *There* were the saints who, under intolerable pangs, had glorified God by meek submission to his will. And all the time, whilst this tumult of sublime memorials held on as the deep chords from some accompaniment in the bass, I saw through the wide, central field of the window, where the glass was uncolored, white, fleecy clouds sailing over the azure depths of the sky: were it but a fragment or a hint of such a cloud, immediately, under the flash of my sorrow-haunted eye, it grew and shaped itself into visions of beds with white lawny curtains; and in the beds lay sick children, dying children, that were tossing in anguish, and weeping clamor-

which is in the midst of the paradise of God.

ously for death. God, for some mysterious reason, could not suddenly release them from their pain; but he suffered the beds, as it seemed, to rise slowly through the clouds; slowly the beds ascended into the chambers of the air; slowly, also, his arms descended from the heavens, that he and his young children, whom in Palestine, once and forever, he had blessed, though they *must* pass slowly through the dreadful chasm of separation, might yet meet the sooner. These visions were self-sustained. These visions needed not that any sound should speak to me, or music mould my feelings. The hint from the litany, the fragment from the clouds, — those and the storied windows were sufficient. But not the less the blare of the tumultuous organ wrought its own separate creations. . . . . . Sometimes I seemed to rise and walk triumphantly upon those clouds which, but a moment before, I had looked up to as mementos of prostrate sorrow; yes, sometimes, under the transfiguration of music, felt of grief itself as of a fiery chariot for mounting victoriously above the causes of grief."

REMEMBER,
  Heaven will be inherited by every one who

She hath received a glorious kingdom.

has heaven in the soul. "The kingdom of God is within you."[145]

    Happy we are!
    For though we stand alone,
    Like the disciples gazing up to Heaven,
    Toward our ascended one,
    We know that God, who takes what he has given,
    Never a soul forsakes,
    And surely gives again that which he takes.
    He who has passed above the sky
    Has gone in time, comes in eternity.

    .   .   .   .

    His young feet pressed death's portal without fear,
    To lift our deathlike thoughts and bring Heaven near.

        No creeping doubts perplexed us,
          In those life-laden hours;
        The boy lay teaching better things,
          A flower begirt with flowers.[173]

REMEMBER,

There are moments in the Christian life upon which the spoil of a long conflict seems heaped, in which it can rejoice even with the joy of a late yet abounding harvest. . . . . . Light is good, and it is a pleasant thing to behold the sun. Yet far dearer than outward peace, far sweeter than inward consolation, is that the ever-during stay, the solace of the Christian's heart, the imperishable root of which all else that gladdens it is but the

And a beautiful crown from the Lord's hand.

bloom and odor; the dry tree that shall flourish when every green tree of delight and desire fails. It is to the Cross that the heart must turn for that which will reconcile it to all conflicts, *all* privations; which will even enable it, *foreseeing them*, to exclaim, "Yet more." . . . . . Let this powerful attraction be once felt, the heart's, the world's great and final Overcoming, and all other bonds will weaken, all other spells decay. "*Midnight is past,*" sings the sailor on the Southern Ocean. "*Midnight is past, the Cross begins to bend.*" "Thou art gone up on high; thou hast led captivity captive."[50]

REMEMBER.

The glory of our promise is "unspeakable." Conceive a translation to Heaven, and a return from thence. How would a man describe the things seen and heard? In the fourth chapter of Revelation the attempt is made, but it instantly takes the form of symbols and figures. A throne is there, and One is there like a jasper and a sardine stone; a rainbow like an emerald encircles all. Seven Spirit Lamps are burning; the lightnings and thunderings and voices are heard, and the sea of glass shines like a crystal. Thus did the

All things work together for good to them that love God.

writer in high symbolic language attempt, inadequately, to shadow forth the glory which his spirit realized, but which his sense saw not. For heaven is not scenery, nor anything appreciable by ear or eye. Heaven is God felt. God dwells in thick darkness. Silence knows more of Him than speech. His Name is Secret; therefore beware how you profane His stillnesses. To each of His servants He giveth "a white stone, and in the stone a new name written, which no man knoweth saving he that receiveth it."[147]

Remember,

Man is higher than his place; he looks upward and uncloses the wings of his soul; and when the sixty minutes, which we call sixty years, have finished striking, he arises and kindles whilst he mounts, and the ashes of his plumage fall back, and the unveiled soul arrives alone, without earth, and pure as music, on high. But here, in the midst of his darkened life, he sees the mountains of the future world standing in the morning-gold of a sun which, here below, does not ascend. Thus the inhabitant on the North Pole, in the long night, when the sun no longer rises, espies, nevertheless, at twelve o'clock, a morning-red

Is it well with the child? And she answered, It is well.

gilding the highest mountains; and he thinks on his long summer, wherein the sun never sets.[34]

    Nosegays! leave them for the waking!
        Throw them earthward, where they grew;
    Dim are such beside the breaking
        Amaranths he looks into;
Folded eyes see brighter colors than the open ever do.

    We should see the spirits singing
        Round thee, were the clouds away;
    'T is the child-heart draws them, singing
        In the silent-seeming clay, —
Singing! Stars that seem the mutest go in music all the way.

www.ingramcontent.com/pod-product-compliance
Lightning Source LLC
Chambersburg PA
CBHW021841230426
43669CB00008B/1038